To my husband, Sam D. Starobin, and our grandchildren,
Phelan, Jesse, Zachary, Rachel, and those to come

The Other Victims

First-Person Stories of Non-Jews Persecuted by the Nazis

Ina R. Friedman

Houghton Mifflin Company
Boston

Library of Congress Cataloging-in-Publication Data
Friedman, Ina R.
  The other victims: first-person stories of non-Jews persecuted by the
Nazis / by Ina R. Friedman.
      p.   cm.
  Includes bibliographical references.
  Summary: Personal narratives of Christians, Gypsies, deaf people,
homosexuals, and blacks who suffered at the hands of the Nazis before
and during World War II.
    HC ISBN 0-395-50212-8   PAP ISBN 0-395-74515-2
    1. World War, 1939–1945 — Personal narratives — Juvenile literature.
2. World War, 1939–1945 — Atrocities — Juvenile literature.   3. World
War, 1939–1945 — Participation, Juvenile — Juvenile literature.   4.
World War, 1939–1945 — Europe — Juvenile literature.   5. Persecutions
— Europe — History — 20th century — Juvenile literature.   6. Youth —
Europe — Biography — Juvenile literature.   [1. Holocaust survivors.
2. World War, 1939–1945 — Personal narratives.]   I. Title.
D811.A2.F74   1990
940.53'161'0922 — dc20   89-27036
[B]   CIP
[92]   AC

Printed in the United States of America
QUM   10 9 8 7

Acknowledgments

The writing of any book is always an inner and an outer journey. In this adventure, I was fortunate to be accompanied by my husband, Sam D. Starobin. He served as translator, interpreter, and researcher.

Our search for interviewees took us to various parts of the United States and to Germany. Wherever we went, we were graciously received. In addition to those individuals whose stories are included in the book, there were many others who consented to be interviewed or who helped in developing our understanding of the enormous numbers and categories of people affected by the Nazis.

Dr. Richard Hiepe of the Neue Muenchner Galerie in Munich provided us with material on artists under the Nazis.

Conversations with Fred Pernell and Hans Massaquoi helped in researching sources on blacks and the Nazis.

For the story on the Pastors' Barracks, I am indebted to Dr. Robert L. Wise for permission to use material from his book, *The Pastors' Barracks*, SP Publications, 1986. Additional material was obtained on our visit to Dachau from the director, Dr. Barbara Distel; Dr. Angelika Pisarski; and the Carmelite Sisters. The Reverend Aram Marashlian also permitted me to read his dissertation on the Reverend Martin Niemoeller.

Dr. Horst Biesold generously made his files on the deaf and the Holocaust available to us and arranged several interviews. Janice Cagen Teuber and Hartmut Teuber, Director Victor Bartl, Gene Bergman, David Bloch, Wolfgang Czempin, Frau Barbara Fiedler, Valerie Sears, Simon Carmel, Fridolin Wasserkampf, and Director Manfred Wloka, among others, aided us in finding deaf individuals who had been sterilized to interview.

The material for the story on Jehovah's Witnesses was obtained from the United States Holocaust Memorial Museum Archives, RG-32, Religious Victims, Sub-collection 02 Jehovah's Witnesses, Kusserow Papers. Dr. Brewster Chamberlain and Mr. John Ferrell of the Museum Archives were extremely helpful. Elizabeth Dopazo provided further information on Jehovah's Witnesses.

Dr. Ian Hancock of the World Romani Union has been of enormous assistance. The Honorable Bill Duna of the U.S. Holocaust Commission, Illunia and Daniel Felczer, Mr. Andreas Freudenberg, Leita Kaldi, Dr. Kay King, Dr. Donald Kenrick, Dr. Jan Kochanowski, and Dr. Gabrielle Tyrnauer also made valuable suggestions concerning the Romani (Gypsy) Holocaust.

Dr. Susanne Miller and Dr. Dieter Dettke provided me with information on political opposition to the Nazis.

For the story on the secret medical school and background material on the Polish underground I am indebted to Alex Adler, Dr. John L. Parascandola, Dr. Witold Rudowski, and Felicia Strojny.

Annegret Ehmann provided us with information not only on the German Resistance but also on the racial policies of the Nazis. The members of the Bontjes van Beek family provided insights into anti-Nazi activities during World War II.

Special thanks are due to Annie Thompson, who was kind enough to serve as sounding board during the writing of this book.

I am indebted to Dr. Jack Nusan Porter for permitting me to read his translation of Professor Ruediger Lautmann's book, *Pink Triangle: The Social History of Antihomosexual Persecution in Nazi Germany.*

In addition, Sybil Milton and Susan Morgenstern of the United States Holocaust Memorial Museum were extremely helpful, as were Rabbi Eugene Lipman, Rabbi Ronne Friedman, Dr. Bill and

Margurite Knisely, Barbara Roberts, Sonia Weitz, Thelma Gruenbaum, Dr. Mary Johnson of Facing History and Ourselves, Adaire Klein of the Simon Wiesenthal Center; Linda Hurwitz of the Holocaust Center of the United Jewish Federation of Greater Pittsburgh; Nora Levin of the Holocaust Awareness Museum of Delaware Valley; and Harriet Wacks and Zelda Caplan of the Holocaust Center of the North Shore Jewish Federation.

My thanks to all of them, and a very special thanks to my editor, Matilda Welter.

My apologies to anyone I have inadvertently omitted.

Contents

Introduction

Fifty years after the Holocaust many people believe that only Jews were the victims of the Nazis. That is not true. While six million Jews were killed in the Holocaust, five million Christians were also deliberately murdered by the Nazis.

Who were these other victims and why were they persecuted?

To understand the fate of these millions, it is necessary to examine the Nazis' master plan for world domination. This plan detailed with great precision how other nations would serve the German so-called Master Race.

For some — Jews, Gypsies, blacks, and most Slavs — there was no place in this new world order. All others had a function: some as slaves, others as obedient servants. For those who did not wish to serve the Master Race, who wished to be free to live their own lives, to think their own thoughts, there was no place. They too would be eliminated.

The theory of the Master Race had been in existence in other countries, as well as Germany, long before Hitler and his Nazi government came to power. For many years, some scientists and educators had been teaching that certain races of people were superior to others. They believed that this Master Race, composed of white, blue-eyed, blond-haired individuals, had the right to rule over and enslave "inferior" races. They called this Master Race Nordic or Aryan. For generations Germans had been taught the legends of the ancient Germanic gods and heroes. These stories praised war and conquest. One popular legend proclaimed that one day a strong man would come to lead the German nation to its rightful place as the ruler of the world.

The Germans wanted to believe these legends. After World War I, the Germans were desperate. They had suffered a humiliating defeat at the hands of the Allies. Their proud armies were disbanded. The country was in a terrible economic depression and millions of people were out of work. The government was unable to keep order.

When Hitler came to power in January 1933, he was welcomed by most Germans. He seemed to be the strong man they were waiting for. He promised to restore German pride and power, to create jobs and bring about prosperity, to drive out and punish the people who he claimed had caused Germany to lose the war, and he promised to unite the "real" Germans.

What the Germans did not realize was the price of this kind of unity: mental and physical enslavement. Hitler's unity meant following him blindly, never questioning his actions, never thinking for themselves. Anyone who was different or posed a threat to Nazi unity was to be wiped out.

In politics, there was one party — the Nazi party. All others were banned. The freedom of the ballot box and the right to express a personal opinion were dead. The only voice allowed was that of Hitler and his thugs.

In religion, the Christian belief in love and mercy was to be wiped out. A pagan religion based on blood and conquest would take its place. Loyalty would be sworn only to Hitler.

In the arts, Hitler would decide what artists should paint, what music was to be performed, and what plays and books would be produced. Anyone who did not conform could not practice his art. Art was to be used as propaganda to reinforce and broadcast Nazi theories.

In his attempts to build a Master Race, Hitler was determined that only the physically fit would be permitted to have children. The mentally and physically handicapped were either to be sterilized or killed. Blacks and homosexuals were to be eliminated.

The plans extended to other nations. Some countries would be swallowed up in the German empire and their people enslaved. Others, like Holland and France, would have puppet governments. They would be allowed to have their own leaders and run their own affairs only as long as they blindly obeyed the orders of the Germans.

The personal stories that follow illustrate the Nazis' control over the lives of non-Jews. In many cases, these individuals were persecuted not for individual acts against the Nazis, but because they did not or would not conform to the racial or political theories of Hitler's police state.

The stories are about survival, but I hope the reader will bear in mind that for each person who survived, many others did not live to tell their stories. They were killed by starvation, disease, brutality, or in the gas chambers. They were victims of a systematic plan to get rid of all opposition to the Nazi regime.

The stories of the young men and women in this book are remarkable. They demonstrate a tremendous will to live, enormous courage, and the blessing of good luck. They are an inspiration for all of us.

PART I
Those "Unworthy of Life"

1

Bubili: A Young Gypsy's Fight for Survival

Persons under protective arrest, Jews, Gypsies, and Russians . . . would be delivered by
the Ministry of Justice to the S. S. to be
worked to death.
— Order issued by Heinrich Himmler, September 18, 1942

Even though they are the descendants of ancient tribes
from Northern India, the Romani were called Gypsies by
Europeans. The Europeans thought they had migrated
from Egypt because of their dark skin and did not seem to
realize that the Romani were composed of several tribes,
the largest being the Sinti and Roma. Grouped into one
category, "Gypsies," they were persecuted throughout the
centuries. In this, the Germans were no exception.

Of all Hitler's intended victims, only Gypsies and Jews
were to be exterminated completely. No member of these
groups, from infants to grandparents, was to be permitted
to live. To justify their complete destruction, the Nazis labeled them socially "inferior," "racially impure," and "criminals." German scientists were ordered to conduct sham
medical experiments to prove the Gypsies' inadequacy by
measuring their skulls. Other medical experiments were
created to demonstrate falsely that Romani blood was different from so-called normal blood. These absurd claims

7

were hailed by the Germans who wanted to believe in their own superiority.

The Romani, like the Jews, were natural scapegoats. Both groups were outsiders, the Jews because they were not Christians, the Romani for various reasons. When the dark-skinned Romani first arrived in Eastern Europe in the early 1300s (after centuries of migration from their native India), they appeared strange to the Europeans. They spoke a language unlike any other ever heard in Europe. Since they could not claim land that was already occupied, they lived in wagons. Because they had come via Turkey, Europeans thought they were Muslims. They were not. Neither were they Christians. When they adopted Christianity to conform to the country in which they lived, they still held on to their Romani customs. They had their own rules and taboos.

At that time, European craftsmen belonged to guilds or unions. These guilds decided who would be employed. Outsiders, such as Jews and Romani, were not allowed to join the guilds. Since they could read and write, the Jews sought other occupations. But the Romani, who were illiterate, had only their ancient trades as armor makers, basket weavers, musicians, jewelers, and horse traders with which to earn a living. The superiority of their work made them a threat to local craftsmen. Because they were kept out of the marketplace, many Romani had to live by their wits.

Even when they attempted to join the church, they were not welcome. Their fortunetelling and "ability to predict the future" made the priests fear them. In the Middle Ages, the uneducated peasants were very superstitious. The church wanted the people to believe only what the priests told them. The church did not want the Romani giving people other forms of hope or fear.

While they were feared by competitors and despised as a people, the Romani were prized for their skills. In the Balkan countries, they were enslaved in the fourteenth century by monasteries and landowners and it was not until the nineteenth century that slavery was abolished in eastern Europe.

To escape oppression, many Romani fled to western and northern Europe in the fifteenth century. However, as soon as they arrived, the various countries passed laws to keep them out. Rewards were offered for Gypsies, dead or alive. In some places, if a Gypsy woman was discovered, her left ear was cut off. Gypsy hunting was an accepted pastime. In nineteenth-century Denmark, one hunt "bagged" 260 men, women, and children.

Hatreds do not easily disappear. The foundations for the Nazis' policies against the Romani were laid in 1899, long before Hitler came to power. A "Central Office for the Fighting of the Gypsy Menace" was established in Munich. By 1920, all Romani were forced to be photographed and fingerprinted because of their so-called criminal tendencies.

The Nazis' first proposal to rid Germany of the "Gypsy Menace" was suggested in 1933. Thirty thousand Romani were to be sent out to sea and the ships sunk. Fortunately, this plan was abandoned. However, many Romani were sterilized at that time. The sterilizations were carried out under a newly passed law permitting the sterilization of "mentally defectives."

In 1935, under the Nuremberg Laws, Jews and Gypsies

were declared second-class citizens. Any individual who had two Romani great-grandparents out of eight great-grandparents was declared a Gypsy. Many of these people had been assimilated into the German population and were unaware of their Romani heritage.

In 1936, four hundred Bavarian Romani were sent to the Dachau concentration camp. Mass roundups of Sinti began in 1938. Some of those rounded up had sons in the German army. By March 1939, the law required all Romani to register at the "Central Office for the Fight Against the Gypsy Menace." The invasion of Poland brought orders to the *Einsatzgruppen* (the Nazi extermination units) to round up and murder all Gypsies, Jews, and Poles. Like the Jews, the Gypsies were moved into special areas and prevented from leaving. In 1940, a group of 250 Gypsy children from Brno, Czechoslovakia, were taken from their parents and used in an experiment to test the efficiency of Cyklon B, a poisonous gas.

All Sintis serving in the German army were removed from their units and sent to Auschwitz in 1942. Some arrived in uniform wearing the medals they had received for bravery. Most were gassed.

The Sinti and Roma who were not gassed were used in medical experiments. These included different methods of sterilization, without the use of anesthesia.

In Dachau, Romani were among the inmates used to determine how much salt water an individual could drink before dying. At Auschwitz, Dr. Josef Mengele used Gypsy twins for inhuman and scientifically unfounded experiments. He sent their organs to Kaiser Wilhelm Institute in Berlin for dissection.

At least half a million Romani were murdered by the Germans. As more and more Nazi records are discovered, the number grows. Countless others bear the scars of physical experiments and mental anguish caused by their own suffering in the camps and by the loss of their families. Unfortunately, the persecution of the Romani continues. The West German government has never acknowledged the suffering of the Romani during the Holocaust. As of this writing, it has never paid reparations for the suffering of the Romani. Laws restricting the movements of the Romani are in effect in many lands. Even in the United States, some states still require Gypsies to be licensed.

The treatment of the Gypsies throughout the world is a continuing shame to all nations. Anton Fojn's story mirrors the treatment of the Romani by the Nazi government.

———•———

I cried when the prison barber clipped my hair and threw the locks into my lap. "A souvenir, Gypsy." At sixteen, I was very vain. My black wavy hair had reached to the nape of my neck. How could the Germans do this to me, Bubili, an Austrian Sinti? The barber put his hand on my shoulder to keep me from rising. "I'm not finished." With a dull razor, he shaved the rest of my head, my chest, my whole body. When he finished, my whole body ached. I stared at those standing next to me. My father, my uncles, and my cousins were unrecognizable, plucked birds from some strange planet.

And I? Without my hair, I was no longer Bubili. I was a piece of wood.

No, worse. Even a piece of wood could be used for

something. We were trash, something to be thrown away. Why did the Germans have to strip us of our humanity?

The commandant and the S.S. men came into the room. They poked us as though we were cattle. "These Gypsy men are strong. Not like the Jews and the others who come here half starved. Why not send them to the army? Let them learn to fight for us."

"Orders are orders," the commandant said. "Treat them like the rest of the scum."

How did I arrive at Dachau concentration camp? I had never heard of the place.

When Hitler marched into Austria in March 1938, he first entered Linz and Vienna. I couldn't read. I wasn't aware of what the Nazis were doing in those cities. I lived in Klagenfurt, in southern Austria. For a few days, nothing happened.

One night, I went to the movies. Before I entered the theater at seven o'clock, I heard people shouting "Heil Schuschnigg." Schuschnigg was prime minister of Austria before the invasion. At nine o'clock, when I came out, people were yelling "Heil Hitler."

I stopped a man on the street. "What kind of a cattle call is 'Heil Hitler'?"

"Be quiet," the man whispered. "The Germans have just entered Klagenfurt. You'd better go home as fast as you can. Stick to the side streets. Don't let them see you."

My father was relieved when I walked into our house. "Bubili, I don't want you going into the center of town. We have to learn what the Germans have in mind for our people," he said. My father could read. He knew about Hitler's threats.

I was fifteen. I couldn't understand what was going on. When one of my uncles was taken to the hospital, I set out to bring him some food. As I walked toward the *Lindwurm-platz*, I noticed men in long leather coats talking to the police. I didn't know a Gestapo from a giraffe. An Austrian policeman grabbed me by the arm. "Hey, dark one, where are your papers?"

"My father has them. Come with me to my house."

Instead, he threw me in jail.

"Why are you locking me up? I haven't done anything."

"The Germans are the authority here. I don't know why they want you. Perhaps they'll send you to Germany, to a concentration camp." The policeman slammed and locked the cell door.

I looked at the other prisoner. "Tell me, please, what does 'concentration camp' mean? The policeman thinks the Germans want to send me there."

The prisoner looked frightened. He shrank into the corner, as though I was poison. "It's a death camp."

"Death camp? I have to escape." I looked around. The only opening was a narrow window with bars. It overlooked the exercise yard.

"It's impossible," the other man said. "No one can escape from this cell. You're a dead man."

"No, I am Bubili."

The cell door opened, and the guard shoved in a drunk. "I know, I know, there are only two cots, but he'll be gone by tomorrow."

The drunk collapsed on the floor and started to snore. I

13

searched his pocket for cigarettes and found a knife. As he slept, I moved the knife back and forth across the radiator to make sharp teeth like a saw.

In the morning, the guard removed the drunk. I poked around the mortar surrounding the window. "There's wood here," I whispered to my cellmate. "Lie down with your ear to the floor. Whistle if you hear the guard coming."

The guards went around in felt slippers. You could only hear them if you kept your ear to the floor.

I worked like crazy, moving the knife back and forth until I made a hole alongside the window. I sawed until it was big enough for my head to go through. I was slim and wiry. Late that night, the other prisoner followed me through the hole onto the tin roof. It was raining, and the sound of the rain on the roof dulled all other noises. I hung from the roof by my hands and dropped to the ground. The other man followed. I led him through the back alleys to the woods. For several days we walked until we came to the Yugoslavian border. My father and I had crossed over into Yugoslavia many times with our racehorses. Father was also a violinist. He played in taverns in towns on both sides of the border so I was familiar with the area. When we came to the outskirts of Slovenia, I cautioned my companion, "If we bump into a policeman, act natural. For God's sake, don't panic and run."

A few blocks from the border, we saw a policeman patrolling the street. Right away, the other guy took off. Before I knew it, we were behind bars again. How could I get out of this prison? When the guard opened the door the next day, he said, "Go back where you belong, Gypsy," and led us to the Austrian border.

I was afraid to go home. Instead of returning to Austria, I made my way toward another section of the Yugoslavian border. I was used to surviving in the woods. I caught rabbits and squirrels and roasted them over a fire. For months I lived on the run in Yugoslavia, in and out of prison. Eventually I decided Yugoslavia was too hot for me, and I went to Hungary. There, I met a Sinti who had lost his wife. I took care of his two young children while he worked. In the evenings, I went to taverns where there were Sinti musicians and danced to earn money. I had studied ballet and was a good dancer. One night the police burst into the tavern. The musicians stopped in the middle of their song.

"Line up, Gypsies." The policeman shouted.

The musicians stood there with their instruments. Romani who had come to hear them were arrested, too. We were marched toward the railroad station. As we stood there waiting for a train, I darted into a crowd of people. The police were afraid to shoot. I jumped into the Danube River and swam until it was safe to go ashore.

Dripping wet, I entered a tavern across the border in Bratislava, Czechoslovakia. "Where God wills," as we say, "one meets Gypsies." After the tavern closed, I walked down the street and met four Gypsy musicians returning home from an evening's work.

"Ah, Bubili, we know your father," the violinist said. "Stay with us until we can find news of your family."

Months passed, but none of the Romani who traveled past the campsite had heard anything.

"I'm going back," I told my friends. "I have to know what is happening to my family."

"It might not be safe," my father's friend said. "It's unusual for our network not to have any news. Stay with us."

It was 1939. I had been away from home for more than a year. I "borrowed" a bicycle and arrived in Graz, Austria, around midnight. At the *Gasthaus Hasenwirt*, I went to the owner. We had always stopped at this inn to take care of the horses. "Where is my family?"

"Bubili, I don't know. The Germans have locked up many Sinti. But I think there are still some at Bruck an der Mur. Your father may be among them."

Bruck an der Mur was in the Austrian Alps, a good thirty-five miles away. I left immediately, using the darkness to make my way through the streets into the forest. I dared not be seen. A day later, I reached our circle of wagons high in the mountains. My uncle was astonished to see me. "Bubili, we thought you were dead."

My father, my grandmother, my uncles, and my aunts crowded around to hug me.

After my grandmother had fed me some stew from the kettle, I lay down to rest. "Tomorrow," my father said, "go to your mother's brother in Leoben. I think you will be safer there." My mother had died two years earlier.

The next morning, I hiked through the mountains to Leoben, beside the river. My mother's family welcomed me. That night, my uncle and I went to a tavern. As the tavern owner shook my uncle's hand to welcome him, he whispered, "Blauch, take off. A drunken policeman boasted of a Gypsy roundup tomorrow. You'll all be sent to a concentration camp."

"The Germans can't do anything to us. We are Austrian citizens," my uncle assured me, "but, Bubili, let's get back to the wagons." The gaily painted wagons were grouped around the foot of a hill. At the top of the hill, there was a shed. Instead of sleeping on the ground next to my uncle's wagon, I took some quilts and went to sleep in the shed.

The next morning, June 26, 1939 (I can never forget the date), S.S. and Austrian police surrounded the wagons at daybreak. My aunt tried to signal me to leave. She sang as loudly as she could in our Romani language. "Bubili, run." But when one is young, one sleeps so well. When I did not wake up, she sang louder, "Run, run, the police are here. The Deathheads have come."

I grabbed my pants and started to jump out the door. A waiting S.S. man seized me. "You," he said, pushing me down the hill, "join the others."

"I'll help my uncle take the horses out of the stall so the horses can pull the wagon to the police station," I said.

"No," the S.S. man said. "Leave them in the stable. You'll pull the wagon yourself."

My uncle had only one leg. My aunt and I and two other Sintis harnessed ourselves to the wagon. Just outside the city, I tried to dart away. But the S.S. man grabbed me. The courtyard of the police station was already crowded with so many Sinti that we stood there like herrings crammed into a barrel.

While the police were registering the men, my aunt whispered, "Bubili, hide beneath my petticoat." Our women wore three and four skirts that touched the ground. I was very thin and agile and could easily have hidden.

"I can't. Uncle has only one foot. I have to help him."

The next day, the Germans forced all the men to climb

17

into busses and trucks. I was the only young boy among 1,035 men. The women and children were released to go home. Where was my father?

My father had been picked up in an earlier raid on Bruck an der Mur. At the railroad station, he found out that my uncle and I had been taken. He asked the Germans to let us travel in the same boxcar. Two days later, June 28, the train stopped just outside the gates of Dachau. We waited, locked in the airless boxcar for about three quarters of an hour. Then we heard a shout as thirty or forty young S.S. men unlocked the bolts and threw open the doors. "Austrian pigheads," they screamed. "Out, out. Run, you Congo niggers, run." Their whips fell on us, killing two men as we ran toward the gates of Dachau.

"Line up. Faces to the sun." The whole square was filled with prisoners in striped uniforms. Many of them wore yellow stars on their shirts. The others had different colored triangles on their uniforms.

We stood on the assembly place, the sun beating down on us from early morning until three in the afternoon. If someone dropped, we were not allowed to pick him up. Then an S.S. man with a whip drove us into a building.

"Sit down," the guard said. He held a board with my name and number 34 016 across my chest. The photographer snapped my picture. With his foot, the photographer pushed a lever that punched a nail into my rear. Like a trained monkey, I jumped through the small window leading to the property room. Why couldn't they just tell us to get up instead of punching us with a nail?

In the property room, the guards shouted at us, "Take off all your clothes. Put everything else in the two baskets

— your jewelry, your papers, your money." We stood there naked as the guards led us toward the showers. It was after the shower I lost my hair. I wondered what more could the Nazis do to us?

The prisoners in charge of the clothing laughed as they threw it at us. If you were tall, you got striped pants that were too short. If you were short, you got striped pants that were too long. I would not look any more ridiculous. I "found" thread and shortened my pants.

The shoes were even worse. Only the *kapos*, the prisoners in charge of other prisoners, and the block "elders" had leather shoes. The rest of us were thrown wooden clogs. The wooden shoes hurt and bruised my feet. I had to figure out how to get a pair of leather shoes. It was summer, and we were taken out to help the farmers bring in crops. At the risk of my life, I smuggled potatoes in my shirt into camp. The big commodity was *schnapps* (whiskey). By bartering, I got *schnapps*, which someone had stolen from the S.S. The *schnapps* I traded for leather shoes. We Romani have always been concerned about our hair, our teeth, and our shoes.

Inside Dachau, the prisoners were a mixed lot. The triangle on his uniform marked each man. Gypsies had brown triangles; political prisoners, red. The greens were the most feared. They were criminals who had been sent to Dachau. Often they were the block elders or worked in the administration. Jehovah's Witnesses wore purple triangles; homosexuals, pink. The Jews had two yellow triangles arranged into a Jewish star.

In September 1939, Germany invaded Poland and World War II began. Many of us were shipped to Buch-

19

enwald. Little did I know that I would consider Dachau heaven compared to Buchenwald. In Buchenwald, everything had to be done on the run. "*Schnell, schnell* (faster, faster)," the guards shouted as we struggled to haul trees or dig trenches. Blows fell on our backs and necks. One of my uncles could not move quickly enough. An S.S. man bludgeoned him to death.

Every night, I fell asleep with a pain in my heart. I kept saying to myself, "I am Bubili. I will outlive those bastards. I will one day give testimony." I prayed for the luck that would help me to stay alive.

One morning, as we stood at roll call, shivering in the snow, the S.S. man shouted, "Everyone count out loud from one to seven. Every seventh man step forward." My father was lined up next to my mother's youngest brother. I was near the end of the line.

I began to sweat. Out of the corner of my eye, I tried to figure out whether my father and uncle were safe. I heard my father shout "Five." I breathed a sigh of relief. The counting grew closer. "Three," the man next to me called. "Thank God." I had survived the selections for death this time.

In December 1941 all Austrian Gypsies were shipped to Gusen 1, a labor camp in Austria. There, I was put in a separate barracks from my father and uncle. By luck, I had a good *kapo*. But I was concerned about my father. Though he was a powerful man, much taller than I, he had been weakened by lack of food. One day, when I returned from a work detail, I went looking for him. Five times I walked past him as he stood in front of his barracks, but I didn't recognize him. He had shrunken to half his size. I finally recognized him by his big nose. I was shocked when I realized his physical condition. I lifted him in my arms. He was as light as a child.

A week later, the *kapo* assigned me to work in Gross-Rosen, another labor camp. When I saw the Germans were loading my father and one of my uncles onto a truck, I held back, saying, "I want to go with them."

"No, Bubili," the *kapo* snapped. "You go where I tell you."

When I came back that evening, I couldn't find my father. I ran into his barracks. He wasn't there. I ran through the grounds like a madman shouting, "Father, father, where are you?"

My block elder grabbed me. "It's too late, they were gassed on the truck. Calm down, otherwise you're finished."

For several days, I couldn't eat. The block elder talked to me. "If you don't eat, you'll be 'on the road to eternity.' Your father and uncle are gone. You have to do everything you can to stay alive."

Yes, I had to live to bear witness to this senseless machinery of human destruction. Again, I was lucky. The *kapo* helped me to get a job cooking for the S.S. They liked the stews that I had learned to make over the campfires. At last, I had enough to eat. I smuggled out food to the Sinti.

The days and years run together. In six years, I was in a total of ten camps. From hell to hell. In Mauthausen I was put in a punishment camp for fighting with another prisoner. Mauthausen was famous for its quarry with 180 steps, ironically called "the stairway to heaven." The prisoners had to carry stones up the steps. We were so weak, skeletons. The stones rubbed against our skin and left our legs raw. "Run, run, you Congo nigger," the guards shouted, flailing us with their whips. The steps were covered with the blood from wounded prisoners. Those who slipped fell to their death. I always tried to be in the center of the column so if I slipped, I wouldn't plunge over the side.

Toward the end of the war, I was sent to Gusen 2, another labor camp. I was surprised to find Jewish children in the camp. I thought they had all been killed, but here were sixteen children from eleven to sixteen years old. These children had been marked for death. Hitler wanted no one alive to bear witness.

I thought of my brother and my sisters, my nieces and my nephews, and wept. Somehow we had to save these few surviving children. Where they came from, where their parents were, nobody knew. By this time, there was no longer tight supervision in the camps. The younger, highly disciplined S.S. men had fled. Older, less murderous men now held command.

I went to my barracks elder, Juckel. "Juckel, how can we let the Germans murder these children? The war is almost over. They don't have to die."

"But their numbers have already been assigned for the transport to the crematorium. There's no way I can save them. Their numbers are down."

I shook my head. "No, Juckel, there are old people here who won't make it to next week. Trade their numbers for the children's numbers. You can hide the children until the Allies arrive. The new guards don't check like the others did."

He folded and refolded his blanket. "Where would we hide them? It's impossible."

"You're a good man, not like the others. It will be on your conscience," I said, turning toward the door. "Maybe you should talk it over with your friend, the camp elder, in the administration building. Records can be altered."

I went outside and began to play with the children.

Juckel left the barracks. A short while later he touched my arm, "Switch the numbers. If we're caught . . ."

Was I any better than the Nazis deciding who should live and who should die? These were older people, skeletons, barely able to walk. People without hope, *mussulmen* (zombies). Who had the greater right to live? The children or the *mussulmen*? I thought of my sisters and brother.

"Don't say anything," I told the children when I changed their numbers. "Just memorize your new number."

Juckel and the camp elder led the children away. Where they hid them, I don't know.

The fighting grew closer. More and more of the guards disappeared. When the Americans marched into the camp, I was hysterical with joy. I had survived. More than that, I had helped to save sixteen children.

Anton (Bubili) Fojn and his wife live in Hanau, Germany, where he is in the clothing business. They have four grown children. The sixteen children whom he helped to hide em-

23

igrated to Israel. Mr. Fojn is active in the Romani Union. Unlike the Jewish and deaf victims of the Nazis, the Romani have never received any compensation from the German government for their suffering during World War II. Mr. Fojn and the Romani Union are working to correct this inequity.

2

The Pink Triangle: The Nazi War Against Homosexuals

> . . . In our judgment of homosexuality — a symptom of degeneracy which could destroy our race — we must return to the guiding Nordic principle: extermination of degenerates.
>
> — Heinrich Himmler

Throughout history and in almost all societies, homosexuals have been persecuted and held in contempt. Only now are we coming to a more tolerant understanding of homosexuality. We know now that homosexuality is not a disease or a crime but a condition that exists among a significant number of people throughout all societies.

German society, too, had long shunned and persecuted homosexuals. Ancient Germanic tribes condemned homosexuals and buried them in bogs. The laws permitting the death penalty for homosexuality were not abolished in Germany until 1746.

More than a hundred years later, in 1871, Kaiser Wilhelm's government passed Paragraph 175 of the Prussian Penal Code. This law made homosexuality a criminal offense, punishable by imprisonment, and still existed when the Nazis came to power.

In the early days of the Nazi regime, there was an uneasy truce on the subject. While Nazi propaganda described the model Aryan man as tall, blond, strong, and obviously very male, there were contradictory models in the Nazi party. Ernst Roehm, the Nazi bully who founded the S.A., the *Sturm Abteilung* (storm troops or Brown Shirts), was a known homosexual. Roehm and his Brown Shirts had helped Hitler obtain power. They had prevented the disruption of Nazi gatherings and broken up the meetings of other political parties. It was even whispered that Hitler himself was a homosexual. Certainly he was not known to have normal sexual relations with women.

For a long time, Hitler overlooked the homosexual activities of Ernst Roehm, his second in command. Roehm's Brown Shirts had been successful in spreading the Nazi philosophy throughout Germany and had grown from three hundred thousand men when Hitler came to power to three million members in only eleven months. As he grew more powerful, Roehm spoke of taking over the army. He even challenged Hitler's control of the Nazi party. To maintain the support of the army and insure his own rule, Hitler gave orders to eliminate Roehm. Heinrich Himmler, chief of the S.S. (the security police responsible for guarding Hitler and other high officials), carried out the orders. On June 28, 1934, "The Night of the Long Knives," Himmler rounded up and murdered Ernst Roehm and over a thousand of his followers. Others who were seen as a threat to the Nazis were also eliminated. The power of the Brown Shirts was broken, and from then on, the S.S., all of whose members swore personal allegiance to Hitler, was dominant.

In late 1934, the Nazis began their roundups of homosexuals by ordering police departments to submit lists of known gays. Just visiting a gay bar could bring a sentence of six months in jail. Decoys were set up in parks and on the street to attract homosexuals. Arrests followed. Homes were invaded and address books and diaries combed for the names of male friends. The accusation of being a homosexual was used to destroy numerous people who were not gay. When Hitler wanted to eliminate General Werner von Fritsch, who opposed his war plans, Hitler accused the general of being a homosexual. Even though the chief witness confessed he had lied, the general's name was tarnished. He was demoted to the lowest rank of officer.

In cases where the accused were found guilty, many were sterilized or put in prison. Those sent to prison were usually taken into so-called protective custody after they had served their sentence. From there they were taken to concentration camps. Others who were arrested had to choose between deportation to a concentration camp or castration.

Those taken to the concentration camps were forced to wear a pink triangle to identify themselves as homosexuals. Before the roundup of large numbers of Jews, homosexuals and Gypsies were persecuted even more brutally than the political prisoners. Like other groups of prisoners, homosexuals were used for various types of medical experiments. Most of the victims died from these unscientific and crudely performed experiments.

The search for homosexuals was not limited to the civilian population. Himmler gave orders that S.S. men found guilty ". . . will as a matter of course be publicly degraded, expelled, and delivered over to the courts. After serving out their court sentence, they will be brought to a concentration camp on my orders, and while in the concentration camp, they will be shot while attempting escape. . . ." "Attempting to escape" was the excuse given to the families of the S.S. men for their deaths. In the S.S., with its many factions, false accusations were the easiest way to get rid of rivals. After 1943, when every fighting man was needed, the Nazis were less vigilant.

While some lesbians were sent to concentration camps, there were no laws against lesbianism. The Nazis could not believe that German women would be interested in anything other than the production of children.

It is estimated that between five and fifteen thousand homosexuals perished in the camps. After the war, reparations were paid to several groups who had suffered under the Nazis. Homosexual victims were classified as "nonpolitically" persecuted and received no compensation for their suffering.

Fifty years after the Holocaust I was unable to obtain an interview with any homosexual who had been interned in a camp. The life span of the survivors was shortened by their terrible suffering during their internment. Most are now dead.

The prejudice against homosexuals still exists and the few survivors are reluctant to come forward to tell their stories.

PART II
The War Against the Church

3

Pastor Christian Reger:
Barracks 26

We shall have no other God but Germany.
— Adolf Hitler

Adolf Hitler planned not only to conquer the world, but to create a new religion. Instead of pledging loyalty to Jesus Christ, Germans were to obey and pray to Adolf Hitler. This new religion was not based on the principle of "love thy neighbor" but on loyalty to the Nazi ideals: the purity of German blood and a willingness to die for Hitler. The cross, the 1900-year-old symbol of Christianity, was to be replaced by the swastika. The Old Testament was to be discarded, and the New Testament was to be rewritten to incorporate Nazi principles. A book by Adolf Hitler, *Mein Kampf*, was to become Holy Scripture. The old Germanic pagan gods were to be worshiped again. Under the new order, all pastors were to swear allegiance to Adolf Hitler.

Before Hitler could take over the churches, he had to conquer the minds of the German people. The best way to do this was to unite the German people against a common enemy. The easiest target was the Jews.

There is a long history of anti-Semitism, hatred of Jews,

in the German churches. For over a thousand years, Christian clergymen in Germany have felt that everyone should convert to Christianity. Those who did not convert were labeled unworthy human beings.

Except for a small number, the German clergy was happy to go along with the Nazis. The Nazis promised to save Germany from Communism and to make Germany the ruler of the world. The clergy did not know that once Hitler got rid of the Jews, he planned to destroy Christianity.

Outwardly, Hitler promised to protect religion. In 1933, he signed an agreement with the Pope. This "Concordat" promised freedom of religion and granted Catholic officials the right to run their church. But five days after the signing of the agreement, the Nazis abolished the Catholic Youth League. By 1936, all Catholic children had to join the Hitler Youth. The same year, Hitler ordered all crucifixes taken out of church schools in the Muenster area. People who tried to replace the crosses were arrested. Many Germans filled the streets, shouting in protest. The Nazis withdrew the order. In 1937, the Pope issued his only public objection to the Nazis' racial policies. This document, "With Burning Sorrow," condemned the Nazis for not honoring the Concordat; the Pope did not mention the persecution of the Jews. By 1938, Hitler had abolished all Catholic newspapers. The same year, the Nazis tried to burn down the home of Cardinal Faulhaber, who spoke out against the persecution of the Jews. Cries of "Take him to Dachau" reverberated along the street as mobs threw rocks into his windows. The majority of Germany's Catholic priests remained silent. In 1939, the Nazis forbade all religious processions.

The "go-along" policy among the Protestants was equal to that of the Catholic clergy. The Nazi party enjoyed great popularity among the average Germans. Though a few pastors immediately labeled the Nazis' racial theories and actions anti-Christ, most praised Hitler or remained silent. In an attempt to take over the Protestant church, the Nazis organized the German Christian Faith Movement. The movement proposed the abandonment of the Old Testament. The New Testament was to be rewritten as a Nazi document, and Hitler was to replace Christ.

Even though three thousand Protestant ministers joined the German Christian Faith Movement, three thousand others formed the protesting Confessional Church. The rest of Germany's seventeen thousand pastors stood in the silent middle.

Priests, pastors, and nuns in Germany and occupied countries who opposed the Nazis or who tried to rescue or hide Jews or converts were sent to concentration camps. Polish priests were arrested as potential leaders, all of whom were to be eliminated. They were deported to concentration camps. In Dachau, the concentration camp outside of Munich, a special barracks was set up for clergymen, Barracks 26. The nuns were sent to various camps. Other concentration camps also had clergymen, but most were concentrated in Dachau. The majority did not survive the brutality and starvation of the camps.

At least 2,270 priests and pastors from nineteen different occupied countries were sent to Dachau. Those who did survive were terribly weakened by their ordeal. Many did not live long after their release. Christian Reger was one of the few who was able to tell his story.

———•———

For my first sermon in Stegelitz, I wore my Brown Shirt uniform. The congregation burst into applause. Mina, my wife, beamed. Only a few years before, as a young seminary student, I had heard Adolf Hitler speak. Although I did not like his ranting and raving, I saw how much hope he gave the hungry, threadbare men and women in the audience. The huge swastika flags flying from the rafters, the splendidly uniformed soldiers, and the brass band, inspired everyone to stand up and cheer, *"Deutschland erwache! (Germany, awake!)"*

I was proud to be a part of this new nationalistic spirit. In 1932, I wore my uniform to show I was one with the people. Hitler had not yet been elected chancellor, but he promised Germany prosperity and power. A few months after his election in 1933, however, Mina and I were walking in the woods. As we strolled toward our favorite glade, we heard voices. We stopped. A young father, in a Brown Shirt uniform, placed a flag with a swastika across a tree stump. Then, holding up his newborn son, he proclaimed, "I baptize thee, Wilhelm Smit, in the name of the Fatherland and to the glory of Germany."

I was shocked. Baptism was the rite of the church. Christians could only be consecrated to Jesus Christ. There were tears in Mina's blue eyes as we turned back. When we came home, she packed away my uniform. The next

Sunday, I preached about the sacredness of baptism. That night, a terrible banging awakened us. Lights flooded the bedroom window. "Traitors of Germany, traitors of Germany!" voices shouted in the darkness. "*Wir schlagen Sie zusammen* (We'll smash you)."

Petrified, Mina huddled beneath the covers. I crept over to the window and cautiously peeped outside. Young storm troopers, their faces filled with hate, beat their clubs and sticks against the metal truck over and over, rousing the sleeping village. Then it stopped. "This is a warning, Pastor Reger," shouted a voice that had a familiar sound. I heard the motor start and drive off.

"What should we do, Mina?" I asked. "Leave? Stop protesting the teachings of Hitler?"

"What do you want to do, Christian Reger? Keep quiet?"

"Mina, I have to speak up. I can't be silent in the face of evil."

"Then we stay and fight."

It was not easy. There was constant pressure by the Nazis to join the German Christian Faith Movement. The movement had been established by the Nazis to wipe out Christian beliefs. The Old Testament was to be abolished, the New Testament was to be rewritten to praise Hitler instead of Christ. Blasphemy!

Pastor Martin Niemueller, who had been a submarine captain in World War I, organized the Confessional Church. Three thousand Protestant clergy joined the Confessional Church and three thousand joined the German Christian Faith Movement. Eleven thousand Protestant clergymen remained silent.

The years 1933, 1934, 1935 passed. I continued to

preach against the Nazis. As the people became more and more enthusiastic about the jobs the Nazis brought them, the membership in my church grew smaller. Marching bands and huge rallies made the people ignore the persecution of the Jews. After the disgrace of losing World War I, everyone wanted to believe that Germans were superior to other people. One Sunday morning, I stood in the pulpit and pleaded for sanity. "Christianity teaches, 'Thou shalt not kill, thou shalt not steal.' The Nazis preach otherwise. What is the Lord's should remain the Lord's."

With seven hundred other clergymen, I was imprisoned. Suddenly, from all over Germany, people protested our arrests. In a rare instance of responding to public indignation, the Nazis released most of the pastors, including me, but twenty-seven were sent to Dachau.

I could not keep quiet. Every Sunday there was a new outrage. After Crystal Night, the night when synagogues were burned and twenty thousand Jewish men sent to concentration camps, I again protested. "All men are equal in the sight of the Lord." For a second time, I was arrested. After a brief imprisonment, I was released and returned to Stegelitz.

Pastor Niemoeller, too, spent several months in prison. When he was brought to trial, he challenged the Nazi court. "How dare you arrest me? I have always had the best interests of Germany at heart. Hitler is destroying our country."

"I sentence you to a fine of two thousand marks," the judge said. "Prisoner released." As he left the courtroom, the Gestapo rearrested Niemoeller and sent him to *Sachsenhausen*, a concentration camp. I was released and returned to Stegelitz.

Sometimes I wondered how I, a small-town pastor, a

man who had never been a leader, could stand up against Hitler. The only thing I had excelled in, in all my life, was gymnastics. Was I being foolish to go against the tide? But how could I be a soldier of Christ and not fight against the Nazis? Mina agreed.

In 1940, the Gestapo arrested me for a third time. For weeks, I paced up and down the narrow prison cell wondering if I would ever see Mina again. I wasn't allowed to receive any mail. The isolation was frightening and I worried about Mina. Was she all right, or had the Nazis imprisoned her? I grew more and more depressed. One morning, a letter fluttered through the prison peephole. I opened the envelope. Mina had copied, in tiny letters, Acts 4:26–30, ". . . grant unto Thy servants to speak Thy Word with all boldness. . . ." The passage renewed my courage. I would have need of courage, for a few days later, I was sentenced to Dachau.

Like murderers, all prisoners were handcuffed, one to the other. Jews, clergy, Social Democrats, Communists, we marched in forced step to the railroad station. As the group crossed the platform to the waiting cattle cars, a mild-looking man raised his umbrella and began to flail us with it. "Traitors! Whatever the guards do to you won't be bad enough."

How does one describe Dachau? The barking dogs and striking guards, being forced to run through the gates? The photographing, the turning of a man into a number? No longer Pastor Christian Reger, I became 26 661. Even a dog has a name. The shaving of the hair, the beatings, standing there naked while a prisoner in charge of clothing threw out a pair of pants, a shirt, and a hat.

"Number 26 661, what is your crime?" A guard held a box filled with cloth triangles, a section for each color.

"Crime? I'm a clergyman. I am Pastor Christian Reger."

"Political prisoner!" the guard shouted, handing me a red triangle. "Answer only to your number." He shoved a needle and thread in my hand. "Sew the red triangle on your uniform, before you get dressed. You're assigned to Barracks 26, the Pastors' Barracks. De luxe accommodations for clergy." He sneered and struck me on the head.

I reeled as I came out of the administration building and walked toward Barracks 26.

It was 1940, in the year of our Lord. I walked down the main road toward the Pastors' Barracks, Barracks 26. A moat, filled with water, surrounded the camp. Electrified barbed wire encircled the area around the moat. Guard towers, with armed sentries, overlooked each corner of the camp. A terrible stench, as though someone were burning putrid meat, assaulted my nose. I started to choke. What was burning? Dust flew in my face as I walked past the rows of flimsy wooden buildings. I stopped at Barracks 26.

"Welcome to the Pastors' Barracks. I'm Werner Sylten." A small slim man offered me his hand.

"I'm Christian Reger from Stegelitz." As I stood in the "living" area, I saw another room filled with tiers of wooden boards.

The prisoners crowded around me asking for news. They knew that Germany had invaded Poland because there were Polish priests in the barracks.

"Is Germany losing the war?" they asked.

I shook my head. "No, we've taken Norway, Holland, France, Belgium, and Denmark."

Their faces fell. How thin and emaciated they all looked. I turned to Werner. "Why are you here?"

"I had a Jewish grandmother."

Another man came over. "I'm Father Fritz Seitz. I was arrested for hearing the confession of a Pole. Hitler declared Poles subhuman. We're not allowed to give them any rites of the church."

The others told me that when Fritz entered Dachau, a guard seized his rosary and hung it around his head, so it dangled from his forehead like a dancing girl. The guard chased him around the field shouting, "Catholic pig, after the war, we'll get rid of you 'black moles.'"

"There are Catholics in the Pastors' Barracks?"

"Yes, and Greek Orthodox. Hatred knows no discrimination. We come from many countries," Fritz Seitz said.

Everyone went out of his way to warn me: "In the Pastors' Barracks, you can trust your fellow man. Outside, trust no one. People are starving, they will do anything to get an extra crust of bread."

"Roll call," someone shouted.

The men seized their caps. Leonard Steinwender, a priest, took me by the arm. "Twice a day we have roll call in the big square, the *appellplatz*. Never be late. Take off your cap, and stand at attention, no matter how many hours you have to stand there. Stare straight ahead. You'll be beaten, or worse, for any infraction."

That night, I lay on the top tier of the wooden boards, unable to turn over because so many were crowded together. I thought of Mina. Lovely, lovely Mina with her long blonde hair that she usually wore drawn behind her head in a bun. Her sweet, round face seemed to smile at me, calling out, "Have courage." Would I ever see her again?

The next morning, the guards marched the German priests out of the camp. On the other side of the barbed wire, there was a medicinal and herb garden. Our job was to tend the plants. The wind blew dust into my face, intensifying the terrible smell still hanging over the camp. "What is that awful odor? Is there a chemical plant nearby?" I asked Werner Sylten. "It chokes my lungs."

"Humanity," he said, looking straight ahead.

"I'm sorry, I didn't understand you." I walked slowly, my hoe over my shoulder. I was starving. I had had only a piece of bread since I arrived.

"*Schnell, schnell* (faster, faster)," the guards called, lifting their clubs. "You think this is a resort. On the double."

"Those who die of disease or malnutrition or hangings or beatings or from experiments, the Nazis have a long list . . . those who die are burned in crematoriums."

"People are dying?" I was careful not to stop. "But it's uncivilized to kill prisoners. This is a civilized country."

We reached the field. "This is the Third Reich. The Germany that we knew, or thought we knew, is dead. The barbarians are in command." He began to hoe the dry ground.

Fortunately, as a young man I had enjoyed working out in the gym. I was stronger than those ministers who had spent their lives bent over books.

Day by day, my fellow ministers gave me instructions in the art of survival. "Above all, one must have luck. Luck not to be chosen for the hangings, luck not to get sick.

Remember, no matter how ill you feel, do not go to the infirmary."

Werner Sylten nodded. "The Nazis claim they take the sick in invalid transports to a place where the work is easier. They lie. They take them to Hartheim Castle — to be gassed. First they strip them of their eyeglasses, the gold fillings in their teeth, their shoes, clothing. Efficient, godless. I pray daily for their defeat."

My only solace from the starvation and hard labor was our "Chapel." In a corner of the barracks we put two tables together to form an altar. Someone managed to get a white sheet, which we hid when we went out to work. One prisoner, a welder, made a cross and smuggled it into the Pastors' Barracks. In the past, Catholic, Protestant, and Greek Orthodox clergy had been rivals. Now we worshiped together. While hatred reigned outside the barracks, there was brotherhood within. One young man, a deacon in the Catholic church, dreamed of being ordained as a priest. Karl Leitner had round, thick-lensed glasses. He was so frail that I worried that he would not live long enough to be ordained.

Winter came. Heavy snows covered the camp. Since the snow was "heaven" sent, priests and ministers were called out to clear the grounds. I thought I would lose my fingers from frostbite. From daylight to nightfall, the guards shouted, "*Schnell, schnell*. Fill the carts quickly. Do not slacken the pace." We pushed the heavy carts toward the river. I worried about slipping in the snow. If my clothes got wet, it would be easy to get pneumonia.

Somehow, in 1941, a radio was slipped into the barracks.

One morning in December, Leonard Steinwender began to shout, "Hallelujah, hallelujah, praise the Lord! The Americans have entered the war. It will soon be over."

One morning, Werner Sylten was not at roll call. Surprisingly, no fuss was made by the Nazis about finding the missing man. Two days passed as we worried where he was. Then someone found out he was in the infirmary.

"We've got to get him out," I said to Leonard. "They're getting up another invalid transport. Werner wasn't ill. They took him because of his Jewish grandmother."

Three of us rushed silently out the door, walking as quickly as we could without arousing the guards. The windows of the infirmary were dark.

I ran up the stairs two at a time and flung open the door. The beds were empty.

"Who are you?" A voice shouted in the darkness.

"Number 26 661. Where are the patients?"

"Get out, 26 661. They left two hours ago."

I stood there, unable to comprehend.

"Go away, 26 661, or else you'll follow them in the next shipment."

We prayed for Werner's soul as we made our way back to the barracks.

To mark America's entrance into the war, the Nazis cut our rations. The pieces of bread became smaller. We were walking skeletons. Sometimes I wondered how we could go on. Mina's monthly letters helped to sustain me. Each letter contained verses from the Bible to give me hope.

In the summer of 1942, I was so hungry that I plucked some herbs from the garden and put them in my watery soup. I immediately fell to the ground with terrible cramps in my stomach. Out of ignorance, I had eaten digitalis, a drug. My friends carried me to the hospital. A death transport had just left. I was safe for a few days. Even before I was well, I forced myself to stagger out of the hospital.

By the fall of 1942, the barracks were even more crowded. Some of the new inmates were still in their civilian clothes. There seemed to be a new policy of using the prisoners to help the war effort. To make us stronger, we got a little bit more food. My friend Wilhelm Dittner was sent to work in a Messerschmitt factory. I got a job that would save my life. I became a clerk in the payroll office of the S.S.

On Christmas Eve, 1942, we knelt, Catholic and Protestant, on the wooden floor and prayed for our families and our parishes. I thought of Mina. I tried to radiate a special message of love to her. It was the only Christmas present I could send. The loneliness of the years overwhelmed me. I began to cry. I prayed, how I prayed that evil would be no more. I even prayed for our Lord to forgive our oppressors. As I stood up, I felt a great peace. I was a man of God. I would not let my oppressors make me hate.

Even with the death toll, the inmates of the Pastors' Barracks increased. One evening, Hermann Hesse, his head shaved, stood at the door with his son, Helmut. Hermann had been famous for his thick white hair. In their ignorance of Hebrew, the guards had permitted Helmut to keep his Hebrew Bible.

Dr. Hesse looked at the worn faces and emaciated bodies of the men standing before him. "To think, my friends, that Germany has come to this. May God protect us all."

"For years you spoke out, Hermann, and they let you

alone. Why did they arrest you now?" I asked after we had welcomed him.

"At first they let me alone. I had two sons and a son-in-law fighting for the Reich. In 1941, Theodore was killed. Friedrich died a few months ago. After our town of Eberfeld was bombed, I conducted a memorial service. 'This terrible devastation is God's judgment for the terrible things Hitler and his cohorts have done to the Jews. We cannot separate ourselves from the Jewish people.' The next day, the Gestapo arrested us. I fear for Helmut's life. He is not as strong as I."

Early in 1943, Italy fell. Our rations were cut even further. I thought of Mina and struggled to stay alive. Fear leaped upon fear. One of the Polish priests was taken to the infirmary. The Nazi doctors, Claus Schilling and Siegmund Rascher, delighted in using Poles and Russians for experiments.

"They're infecting them with malaria," Hermann Hesse shuddered. "One of the nurses told me."

Early in 1943, Helmut Hesse died from malnutrition. We held a memorial service in the Pastors' Barracks. In the middle of the service, a guard rushed into the barracks, shouting, "Everyone to the washroom." We were not to be allowed the dignity of finishing.

As the months passed, Italy surrendered. More and more prisoners arrived in Dachau. People were in danger of falling off the already overcrowded bunks. Some slept on the floor. Mina wrote that our congregation had dwindled to only a few members. "The pressures against them are tremendous. I cannot condemn them for being afraid for their lives."

Conditions worsened as I began my fourth year in Dachau. One of my best friends in the barracks was Karl Leitner. A Catholic deacon from Muenster, Karl's dream was to become a priest. But by 1944, it appeared that he would die of tuberculosis before he could be ordained. There were no bishops in Dachau to perform the ceremony. I feared that he would not last through the war.

A disaster for one often becomes a miracle to another. In September 1944, the bishop of Clermont-Ferrand, Monseigneur Piquet, was arrested and interned in Dachau. Immediately, the underground network contacted Cardinal Faulhaber and the Bishop of Muenster. The Cardinal entrusted the documents for ordination to a member of the underground. He smuggled them into the camp. Prisoners outside the Pastors' Barracks stole bits of clothing and secretly made the special garments for the ordination. A slave laborer in the Messerschmitt factory surreptitiously welded a ring and a cross. Father Durard, an English priest, magically presented a silk mitre, the priestly hat, adorned with "pearls." Cardinal Faulhaber sent the ritual oil.

Our preparations were so secret that only a few in our barracks knew of the plans for Karl's ordination. If the Nazis had had any inkling, we would have been gassed.

On December 18, 1944, Karl Leitner, frail and flushed with fever, glowed as Monseigneur Piquet placed the vestments over his worn striped uniform. In the dim light of the candles, the spirit of God filled the tiny chapel.

At the completion of the service, Monseigneur Piquet blessed the priestly "banquet," the small dish of Brussels sprouts that had been pilfered from the S.S. kitchen. Karl beamed and took a few bites. "Thank you, my friends, for this glorious day. Forgive me, but I must lie down."

It was a week before the new priest was strong enough to celebrate his first mass.

On Christmas Eve, 1944, I conducted the service. The Red Army had stopped short of Warsaw. Rumania and Hungary had been occupied. There was hope, if only our fragile bodies could survive. In my four years in camp, my weight had dropped from 198 pounds to 99. I began to read from Psalm 50:2–3. "Our God shall come and shall not keep silence."

Day by day the sounds of the guns grew closer. Our brave, swaggering S.S. fled. On April 2, 1945, a policeman entered the barracks. "Relax," he said as we stood stiffly at attention. "Some of you are to be released. I'll call out the numbers of those to be freed."

Everyone surged forward. I stood behind him, trying to read the numbers on the lists. Could it be true? My number, 26 6661, was at the bottom of the second page; 26 6661! I was free. Free to seek Mina. I lowered my head in prayer.

Christian and Mina Reger were reunited in Stegelitz. He was then assigned to a parish in East Berlin. "Because of your imprisonment," Bishop Diebelius said, "you are one of the few clergy the Russians will trust." Mina died in 1970. Pastor Reger died in 1985 at the age of eighty.

4

Elisabeth's Family: Twelve Jehovah's Witnesses Faithful Unto Death

National Socialism is a form of conversion
. . . Once we hold power Christianity will be
overcome . . . and a new Germany without
the Pope and the Bible will be established.
— Adolf Hitler

Why did the Nazis call Jehovah's Witnesses a "degenerate race"? They were white and the descendants of generations of Germans. Many had blue eyes and blond hair. Like Hitler, who professed to be Catholic, they were Christians. They believed in the Bible and the Second Coming of Christ.

Jehovah's Witnesses refused to serve in the German army or navy. Wars between nations did not concern them. The only authority they recognized was Jehovah God, as they called him. The only battle they would fight was on Judgment Day in the war between good and evil. In wars between countries, they refused to take sides.

Jehovah's Witnesses were so firm in their belief that only God should rule the world that they urged other Germans not to fight. The Nazis considered this the action of traitors. The Nazi creed was that every German should be prepared to fight and die for Hitler.

The Witnesses enraged the Nazis further when they refused to salute the flag or to use "Heil Hitler" as a greeting. According to the Witnesses, this would be the same as bowing down to idols.

When the Nazis gained power in 1933, they put Jehovah's Witnesses on a list of groups "dangerous" to the Nazi government. These groups were banned from holding meetings. Jehovah's Witnesses, like the other banned groups, were prohibited from distributing their newspapers and magazines. They weren't allowed to pray, study, sing hymns, or socialize in Kingdom Hall (their meeting place). They were forbidden to gather in private homes.

The search for "subversive" literature began in 1933. Anyone having copies of the *Watchtower* magazine or other religious books was sent to prison. Initially, the Nazis arrested only one parent. They did not want to worry about the welfare of the children of Jehovah's Witnesses. Most Jehovah's Witnesses were released after a few months.

The concern about leaving one parent in the home soon vanished in 1936. If religious literature was found in the home, both parents were arrested for the possession and distribution of forbidden literature. Over eight hundred children were sent to state homes to be raised as Nazis.

To be released from prison, Witnesses had to sign a paper promising not to associate with other Witnesses. Some parents signed, rather than have their children raised in Nazi homes. Most refused to sign. Those who remained in the concentration camps were beaten and forced to do hard labor. Others were beheaded or shot. Some were sent to insane asylums. Many died of starvation or disease. Some of the women sent to Ravensbruck died from rat bites.

By 1939 Jehovah's Witnesses had to wear a purple arm

band to distinguish them from other Germans. Out of the over 25,000 Jehovah's Witnesses who lived in Germany, 6,019 were imprisoned.

The prisoners looked upon their incarceration as something to be endured in their loyalty to Jehovah God.

Elisabeth, the youngest daughter of the Kusserow family, recounts her family's nightmare under the Nazis.

————•————

"Quick, Elisabeth," Annemarie shouted, "the Gestapo!" In Paderborn, very few people besides the Gestapo had cars. The clouds of dust raised by a car coming down the road signaled danger.

Before the Mercedes stopped, I scooped up the *Watchtower* pamphlets and put them in my knapsack. Magdalena stuffed the books into hers. We ran outside and hid the literature behind the bushes. At eight, I knew to walk over to the coops and feed the chickens. Magdalena, who was nine, picked up a bottle to feed the baby lamb.

We were Jehovah's Witnesses. Our parents, Franz and Hilda Kusserow, had taught their eleven children to hide the books and pamphlets of the International Society of Bible Students if anyone spotted the men from the Gestapo coming toward the house. Anyone found with literature from our Watchtower Society could be arrested.

What a happy family we were before Hitler. Our parents had been sent by the Watchtower Society from Bochum, Germany, to Paderborn to set up a congregation of Jehovah's Witnesses. The house sat on three acres of land. Father organized our daily chores. One week the boys took care of the chickens and ducks and lamb. That week, the girls worked in the garden. Then the following week we switched chores. When the apple and pear trees were ripe, everyone helped to pick the fruit.

But it wasn't all work. Before we went to school in the morning, and in the evening, we sat around the table talking about the Bible and what the passages meant. Mother had graduated from teachers' school, and Father made time for her to teach us music and painting. The house was filled with musical instruments: five violins, a piano, a reed organ, two accordions, a guitar, and several flutes. What joyful music we made as we played from the book *Hymns to Jehovah's Praise*.

My father sensed that some of the faithful would be persecuted by Hitler. He talked to us about what it meant to be a Jehovah's Witness. Sometimes he quoted from Matthew and Revelations. "Fear none of those things which thou shalt suffer; . . . be thou faithful unto death, and I will give thee a crown of life."

In 1936, the Nazis tried to get Jehovah's Witnesses to renounce their faith. When the Gestapo knocked on our door, one of them waved a piece of paper in Father's face and shouted, "Franz Kusserow, you must sign this document promising never to have anything to do with the International Society of Bible Students. If you don't, you will be sent to prison."

The whole family stood, dumbfounded. Promise not to be Jehovah's Witnesses? Hitler was truly Satan.

Father read aloud the first paragraph. " 'I have recognized that the International Society of Bible Students spreads a false doctrine and pursues goals entirely hostile to the state under the cover of religious activity.'" Father shook his head. "This is ridiculous. I can't sign."

The S.S. man, who was about the same age as my oldest brother, became angry. "Stubborn fool!"

I was shocked; no one ever talked to Father that way. He was one of the most respected people in Paderborn. The S.S. man turned to Mother. "And you? If you don't, your children will be without parents."

Mother removed her apron and placed it over the chair. "No, I cannot sign. Annemarie" — Mother turned to my oldest sister — "take care of the children."

The agent shoved my parents outside and into the car.

Paul-Gerhard, who was five, began to cry. Hans-Werner, who was six, put his arms around his little brother. Fifi, our dachshund, began to growl. I bent down to calm her and to hide my tears.

After a few days the Nazis released Mother from prison. They kept Father. Why was it a crime to be a Jehovah's Witness? Mother couldn't understand why they released her, because she still refused to sign the paper. Mother and my oldest brother, Wilhelm, made sure we followed Father's schedule and always did our chores. But how we missed Father and his talks about the Bible! What a joyful reunion we had when he was released a year later. All thirteen of us took up our instruments, and the house resounded with hymns of praise. A few months later, our family was shattered. Our brother, Siegfried, who was 21, was killed in an accident.

It was difficult enough losing a brother, but as the years passed, the situation in school became more and more painful. Every day, the teacher reprimanded me for not saluting the Nazi flag. The big black swastika on the red banner flew over the schoolhouse and hung on a pole in every classroom. My stomach churned as I tried to think of how I could avoid saluting it or saying "Heil Hitler." My parents had taught me to salute only Jehovah God. To salute a flag or a person was the same as worshiping idols. I wouldn't sing the horrible Nazi songs, either. I kept my lips together.

The teacher always watched me. "So, Elisabeth, you do not want to join in praise of our leader. Come to the front of the classroom." She turned to the others. "Children, Elisabeth thinks it is all right to insult our leader. Tell us why, Elisabeth."

"Acts 4:12 of the New Testament says, 'There is no salvation in anyone else except Jesus Christ.'"

"Imagine, Elisabeth Kusserow believes in that ridiculous New Testament."

The children laughed. I couldn't understand why. All of them went to church. On the way home from school, they pushed me and threw my books to the ground. It got worse when Hans-Werner and then Paul-Gerhard were old enough to go to school. Now I had to worry about the children tormenting them.

Our troubles grew. It wasn't just the terror of going to school. The Nazis cut off Father's pension from World War I because he still refused to say "Heil Hitler." It was hard doing without the money, even though my older brothers and sisters had jobs. We planted more vegetables and canned as much as we could. In 1938, the Gestapo arrested

Father for a second time. What could be wrong in obeying Jehovah God?

In the spring of 1939, the principal came into my class. "Elisabeth, since you refuse to salute our flag and say 'Heil Hitler,' it is obvious that your parents are neglecting your spiritual and moral development. I have taken it upon myself to obtain a court order to remove you and your two younger brothers from your home. The three of you will be sent to a place where you will get proper instruction." He pulled me into his office. Paul-Gerhard, who was then eight, and Hans-Werner, who was nine, stood there trembling.

At thirteen, the words made no sense to me. "Our parents raised us according to the teachings of Jehovah God," I protested.

"Quiet! This policeman will take you to your new home."

I was so upset, I hadn't noticed the policeman standing next to the window.

"Please, please, let me call my mother." I begged. "She'll be frantic when we don't come home."

"Traitors are not to know what happens to their children."

For several months Mother tried to find out where we were. She went to the police, called orphanages, hospitals, and prisons. Finally, she reached the clerk at the reform school in Dorsten who admitted we were there. Secretly, Mother sent us letters. "Always know that we love you. Be steadfast in your faith to Jehovah God. One day we will be together in heaven or on earth."

The director of the reform school couldn't understand why we were there. "You are the best behaved children I have ever seen. It's ridiculous to have you here with these delinquents." He sent a letter to Mother, "Your children will be arriving in Paderborn on Friday at two P.M."

As we started to climb the steps of the train, two men stopped us. "The director was guilty of misconduct. You are coming with us." They drove us to Nettelstadt, a Nazi training school.

"Don't cry," I told the boys. "Jehovah God will one day rule the earth. We will see our family, either here or in heaven." I didn't feel as brave as I sounded.

At the training school, the teachers became furious when we still refused to salute the flag or say "Heil Hitler." In punishment, the three of us were sent to different places. I kept worrying about Paul-Gerhard and Hans-Werner. They were just little boys.

For six years I remained in the custody of the Nazis, praying that all of my family would survive the war. Was Father still in prison? I kept hearing from my custodians, "Germany is winning the war." Yet how could that be? By 1944, Allied bombers swarmed across the skies, cutting off all other sounds. I held my hands over my ears every time they passed. If Germany were winning the war, why were so many Allied planes able to return to their bases?

One sunny spring morning, I was awakened by songbirds. I ran downstairs. The doors were unlocked. The matron had fled. The war was over! There was nothing to stop me from going home! I said a prayer of thanksgiving and ran to the railway station. The station was jammed with people trying to board the trains. Somehow I squeezed onto the platform between the cars. As the train chugged into the station at Paderborn, I began to have fears. What would I find? Had the boys been forced to go into the army? Was the house still standing?

Would my family recognize me? I had left an awkward teenager. Now I was nineteen. The train stopped. Slowly, I climbed down the steps onto the station platform. I looked at the men and women and children searching the faces of those stepping off the train.

"Elisabeth," three voices shouted.

"Praise Jehovah God," I said aloud as Hans-Werner and my sisters Waltraud and Hildegard ran toward me.

"We've been meeting every train," Hildegard said, her voice breaking, "praying some of us would be on it." She hugged me so hard, I thought my bones would break.

I had so many questions, but I didn't know where to begin. Hans-Werner looked so much like Siegfried, my heart ached. We walked hand in hand toward the house.

I could scarcely recognize my sisters. Waltraud had been in prison for two years. Hildegard was so thin she looked older than Mother had looked when I last saw her. Hildegard had been at the Ravensbruck concentration camp with Mother and Annemarie.

"Somehow we were separated when we were ordered to march out of the camp," Hildegard said. "I don't know where they are."

I half expected Fifi, our dachshund, to come running down the road. But she, like the chickens and ducks and lamb, had vanished.

As soon as I walked into the kitchen, I started to cry. Silence filled a room that had resounded with talk and laughter. I walked into the living room. Our violins and flutes filled the closet. What wonderful harmonious sounds we once had made. I turned to Hildegard. "Tell me everything that happened while I was away. For six years, I've had no news."

Hildegard and Waltraud began to cry. Hans-Werner brushed his tears away with his sleeve. "It was terrible," Hildegard said. "In 1940, Wilhelm was shot for refusing to serve in the army. Mother asked the authorities to permit Father to attend the funeral. By some miracle, he was released. Even in our sadness, we couldn't help noticing how thin and worn he looked. It was such a comfort to have him, if only for the hour of the funeral.

Waltraud nodded. "It was a beautiful funeral. Karl-Heinz read from the Scriptures. But when the Gestapo shouted 'Heil Hitler' at the end of the service, Karl-Heinz refused to return the salute. The Gestapo beat Karl-Heinz and left him on the ground. A few weeks later, they went to the factory where he was working and took him away. We've heard nothing since then."

My head began to ache. Wilhelm shot, Karl-Heinz missing. "And the others?"

"Everyone else was taken away, because we would not renounce our faith. We don't know if the others are dead or alive, except for Wolfgang."

I looked from one face to another.

"When he refused to serve in the army, he was beheaded. It happened on March 28, 1942," Waltraud said softly.

"He was only twenty years old." I couldn't stop trembling.

Hildegard held me in her arms. "Come into the garden,

Elisabeth. Mother hid Wilhelm's and Wolfgang's letters so whoever came back would have them. They have been a great comfort to us."

In the garden where I had once played with the baby lamb, I read aloud Wilhelm's letter. "My dear parents and brothers and sisters . . . You know already how much you mean to me . . . I have been faithful until the death as it is stated in the scripture. . . . It is true that it is difficult to follow this course. . . . But we must still love God above all as our leader Jesus Christ taught. When we stand steadfastly for him, he will reward us. . . ." I put the letter down and began to sob. Wilhelm was only twenty-six.

Among Wolfgang's letters, I found a copy of the defense he had given for refusing to serve in the army. "I was brought up as one of Jehovah's Witnesses according to God's Word contained in the Holy Scriptures. . . . The greatest and most holy law he gave mankind is, 'You shall love God above all else and your neighbor as yourself . . .'

"We are living in a time . . . that has been predicted in the Bible. People today are unbelievers; they do not respect the Bible . . . They ridicule Jehovah's name and say He is a God of the Jews and persecute those who keep God's laws and apply them.

"If Jehovah's Witnesses refuse military service for the reasons above, because God's laws forbid it, they are sentenced to death by the military court, only because they remain faithful to Jehovah and obey Him first. . . .

"For it is better to suffer because you are doing good, if the will of God wishes it, than because you are being evil."

I hugged the letter to my chest. My brothers had left us a great treasure.

Every day we went to the railroad station and to the post office. Things were so chaotic. Most of the railroad tracks had been bombed, and the telephone wires were down. Every night we lay in bed wondering whether the next day's news would be good or bad. One evening, just as I started to fall asleep I heard a great banging on the door. "Hallo, hallo, it's Paul-Gerhard. Open up, I'm home."

I rushed downstairs and fell into his arms. The baby of the family had turned into a sturdy teenager. Unlike those taken to concentration camps, Paul-Gerhard, Hans-Werner, and I had received adequate rations.

One afternoon, a wagon loaded with sheep stopped in front of the house. "Ho, there," the driver cried. "I have a special present. Give me a hand."

We ran outside. Father, whose leg was broken, lay amidst the lambs. The boys carefully carried him into his bedroom. A gift from Jehovah God, when so many parents had been killed. Even from his bed, Father began to organize the household. While we waited for the others, we tilled the soil. Father began to correspond with members of the Watchtower Society overseas.

In July, Karl-Heinz, supported by a nurse, returned from Dachau. My brother, who loved to hike and ride his bicycle before the war, had scars all over his body. He had been beaten by the guards.

The nurse took us aside. "He has tuberculosis. I'm afraid it's too far gone. Do whatever you can to make him comfortable."

Though there was little food, we tried to feed Karl-Heinz as much as we could to give him strength. We prayed that Mother, Annemarie, and Magdalena would see him before he died.

Annemarie, who had been in the Hamburg-Fuhlsbuttel penitentiary, arrived home in July. Part of our prayers had been answered.

It was not until September, four months after the armistice had been signed, that I heard Paul-Gerhard shout, "They're home."

I dropped my hoe. Hildegard, Paul-Gerhard, Annemarie, Hans-Werner, and I ran down the road. What tears of joy as we embraced Mother and Magdalena. The boys lifted their frail bodies in their arms and carried them to Father.

That evening, as we sat around the table, Father raised his voice in thanksgiving. He began with Revelations: "He that overcometh shall inherit all things; and I will be his God, and he shall be my son."

After the war, Elisabeth and Magdalena became special pioneers in the service of Jehovah's Witnesses. Paul-Gerhard became a missionary. Karl-Heinz died of tuberculosis a year after his return from Dachau. Franz Kusserow died in 1950, his life span shortened by the years of imprisonment. Mrs. Kusserow, Waltraud, Annemarie, and Hildegard continued in the work of Jehovah's Witnesses in Germany. Elisabeth died in 1980. Her two children follow in their mother's footsteps.

PART III
Racial Purification: Breeding the Master Race

5

Franziska: A Silent Protest Against Sterilization

The state is a means to an end. Its end lies in
the preservation . . . of a community of physically and psychically homogeneous crea-
tures. . . .
— Adolf Hitler

Hitler did not invent the theory of the Master Race, but
he put these theories into practice. He started by eliminating the "foreign elements" in Germany, the Jews and Gypsies, and by preventing "defective elements" from having
children.

German scientists and educators participated eagerly in
Hitler's program, particularly those at the Kaiser Wilhelm
Institute of Anthropology, Human Heredity, and Eugenics. Eugenics is the study of how hereditary traits can be
altered and "improved." The scientists welcomed Hitler's
attempts to establish the superiority of the German people.
It was profitable for the Institute. They were kept busy
identifying and eliminating inferior non-Germans (Jews,
Gypsies, Slavs, and so on) and German "defectives," the
physically and mentally handicapped.

The cooperative efforts between science and politics began with the "identification" of inferior people. Jewish
schoolchildren's skulls were measured in classrooms to

demonstrate their inferiority. From there the "scientific" methods progressed to sterilization to euthanasia (mercy killing) and finally to mass murder.

Everything was done legally. First a law was passed to remove the "undesirable" elements from public service. Jews lost their jobs as teachers, civil servants, and doctors in hospitals. This decree was followed in July 1933 by the "Law for the Prevention of Offspring with Hereditary Defects." It required that persons who were hereditarily blind, deaf, physically or mentally handicapped, or were alcoholic be sterilized.

A health tribunal was established to decide who would be sterilized. Those called before the tribunal could not examine the documents used against them. Most did not have lawyers for their defense.

Teachers in schools for the deaf, who were themselves hearing, turned over the names of their deaf pupils to the Nazi authorities. From 1934 to 1939, between 350,000 and 400,000 people lost their ability to have children in this unjust and unscientific program.

In 1935 the Nuremberg Laws forbade marriages between Christians and Jews to prevent "race defilement." Many Christians either divorced their Jewish partners or fled the country. Those who remained married to Jews were in danger of being sent to a concentration camp along with their spouse.

With the outbreak of war on September 1, 1939, the Nazis decided that sterilization was an inefficient way to eliminate the mentally handicapped. These "useless eaters" had not only to be fed but housed. With support from the scientists, Hitler directed that a program of "mercy killing" be initiated. In a short time, 75,000 mentally ill and retarded individuals were put to death. The S.S. provided the gassing equipment and the trained personnel. The euthanasia of the mentally ill continued until late 1941. By then the personnel trained in mass killing were needed in the newly established extermination centers. The Nazis then reduced the rations of food and fuel to mental institutions so the inmates either starved or froze to death.

Even before the establishment of the death camps, Germany's conquest of Poland permitted the Nazis to carry out their racial theories. Special killing units (*Einsatzgruppen*) immediately followed the combat troops. The *Einsatzgruppen* were instructed to round up and kill Jews, Gypsies, inmates of mental institutions, and Poles. Jews and Gypsies who were not killed immediately were forced into ghettos to await the Final Solution — death in the scientifically developed extermination centers.

By late 1941, Hitler was ready to put the Final Solution into effect. Extermination centers, principally in Poland, awaited their victims. The S.S., which had perfected its skills in the euthanasia campaign, was prepared to exterminate millions. From all parts of German-occupied Europe, cattle cars filled with "inferior" men, women, and children arrived at the death camps. As soon as they entered the gates of the camps, a selection took place. The healthy and strong were assigned to slave labor until they were worn out. Then they were killed.

Those unable to work — children, the elderly, and most of the women — were sent directly to scientifically constructed gas chambers. The bodies of the thousands killed each day were taken to a special building, a crematorium, to be burned.

The cooperation between the scientists and the government continued in the camps. The Nazis needed doctors to select persons fit to work. The scientists saw an opportunity during the selections to use human "guinea pigs" for their experiments. In Auschwitz, the infamous Dr. Josef Mengele determined who would go directly to the gas chambers, who would work, and who would be used in the experiments.

But he was not acting on his own. He was a member of the Kaiser Wilhelm Institute scientific research team. He sent the products of his investigation (parts of human beings) to the Institute for analysis. The German scientists were grateful.

In 1943, at the height of the mass slaughter in the camps, Professor Eugen Fischer of the Institute wrote to a German newspaper, "It is a rare and special good fortune for a theoretical scientist to flourish at a time when the prevailing ideology welcomes it, and its findings immediately serve the policy of the state." The ethics of murdering human beings did not concern Dr. Fischer.

The Germans came close to winning the war. How much longer would they have continued with their program of exterminating so called "inferior" people?

Dr. Miklos Nyiszli, a slave laborer, was forced to assist Dr. Mengele in the dissection of his specimens. In despair he asked Dr. Mengele, "When will this program of destruction end?"

Dr. Mengele replied, "It will go on and on and on."

Hitler is dead and the Nazi regime is ancient history. But his racial theories are still alive. Many of the German scientists who studied and taught "racial" science continued to teach after the war. The laws for sterilization are still on the books of West Germany.

Today, there are people who say the Holocaust never happened, that it is only an "invention." They are the same people who preach the superiority of the white race and the inferiority of Jews, blacks, Hispanics, and Asians. The Nazi progressed from name-calling, to expulsion from jobs, sterilization, euthanasia, and finally mass murder. Each law, each action affected an individual.

Franziska (Fanny) Schwarz was deaf. When she was sixteen, the Nazis knocked at her door.

I never saw anything wrong with being deaf. My younger sister, Theresa, and most of my friends were deaf. Though my parents were hard of hearing, my younger brother, Theo, had normal hearing. My father was one of six brothers. Four of them were hearing. When they came to visit, every hand was busy sharing news of the deaf community or giving advice. Our eyes were glued to the hands and faces of the signers. Everyone had so much to say.

In deaf school, the teachers got mad if I signed. They wanted me to read lips and to use my voice. I got so tired of watching the teacher's lips. I couldn't look away for a minute. It was even harder when she tried to teach me to say the letters correctly. The teacher put a strip of paper in front of my lips. "To make the *B* sound, purse your lips and blow just enough to make the paper quiver. To make a *P*, blow a little harder and make the paper shake." Day after day, the teacher drilled me.

I felt like a bellows. I liked it better after school when the teachers weren't around. My friends and I would make signs and chat with our fingers.

When I was fourteen, Hitler took over Germany. Theo, my eleven-year-old hearing brother, liked to go to the Munich Stadium to the rallies. Once Theo came home all excited because he had shaken Hitler's hand. My favorite uncle, Karl, who could hear, got mad.

He shouted at my brother and signed at the same time. "Hitler is a disgrace to Germany. Don't waste your time and hearing listening to him."

My father put his fingers on my brother's lips. "Don't ever repeat what you have just heard. Swear by the Holy Father!"

Theo looked scared. "But in school, they tell us to report anything bad people say about Hitler."

"If you don't repeat it, no one will know your uncle said it."

I couldn't hear the radio so I never got excited about Hitler. The year 1933 was hard for me. I had just begun my apprenticeship at the convent. The sisters were teaching me how to sew, and I found it hard to understand them. On Saturdays I enjoyed going to a special Catholic club for deaf girls. Later, Hitler turned it into a branch of the *Bund Deutscher Maedel*, the Nazi club for girls. We went hiking, and once we went on a camping trip to Koenigsburg. That was enjoyable.

The rest of Hitler was horrible. For me, the trouble

started in 1935. I came home from the convent and found Mother crying. "What's the matter?" I signed.

She handed me the letter that read, "Frau Schwarz and her daughter Franziska are to come to the health office to arrange for their sterilization. Heil Hitler." I couldn't make out the signature at the bottom.

The whole family got upset. Uncle Karl started to sputter, as he always did when he was excited. "We'll protest. The Nazis can't do this to Franziska. She's perfectly healthy. I'll appeal to the administrative court ask them to overturn the order."

The day of the hearing, my mother, my father, and all my uncles accompanied me to court. "She's only sixteen years." Uncle Karl talked and signed at the same time so I could understand. "Deafness is not always inherited. I'm her uncle, and I can hear perfectly well. As for her mother, she is going through the menopause. Though she is a good Catholic, she promises not to have any more children."

The two men on the judges' bench whispered to each other. They frowned and shook their heads. After a few minutes, the one with the big nose and bald head stood up. "Petition denied for the minor, Franziska Schwarz. Since the mother promises not to have any more children, she will not have to be sterilized."

I started to cry. The previous year, I had met a boy I liked, Christian Mikus. As a child, he had had scarlet fever and lost his hearing in one ear. Christian and I liked to walk in the park. We'd sign for hours. Whenever he saw children playing, he'd smile and sign, "One day, we will have children, too." Of course we couldn't get married then. He

69

didn't make much money working in a clothing factory. Whatever deaf people made, it was always less than other people. We used to get angry. We'd do just as good work as others, but the employers would always give us less. If I were sterilized, I didn't think Christian would want to go with me anymore.

When my uncle walked out of the courtroom, his face was almost purple. "Franziska, Germany is no place for either of us. We'll run away to Switzerland. I won't let them sterilize you."

Before we could run off, he was arrested by the Gestapo. He had shouted at his secretary, "Turn off the radio whenever Hitler talks. It's not healthy to listen to a madman." The secretary's father was a storm trooper. She reported Uncle Karl to the Gestapo. The Gestapo sentenced him to death for "spreading slander."

I don't know how, but his brothers got him released. "For God's sake. Keep your opinions to yourself. Hitler can't last," my father said. "Why take chances?"

At the same time my uncle was in prison, a letter came from the department of health. "Franziska Schwarz is to report to the Women's Hospital in Munich for the sterilization."

"I won't go," I cried. "I want to be able to have babies."

Father looked sad. "If you don't go, the police will drag you to the hospital."

I screamed all the way to the hospital. The nurse locked me in a room with two other deaf teenagers. The three of us cried all night. When the nurse came to give us tranquilizers, I tried to fight her off. She held me down and gave me the injection. In the morning, I woke up in a room

70

full of beds. My stomach hurt. I touched the bandages and started to cry. The nurse who brought me water was crying, too. "I'm sorry, there's nothing I could do to help you. With Hitler, you have to be quiet." Her finger pointed to the portrait of Hitler hanging over the bed. She tapped her temple with her finger, to indicate, "He's crazy."

I had so much pain, I couldn't go to the convent. I asked the public health insurance office for the standard sick pay.

"Why should you get sick pay?" the social worker sneered. "You can have all the fun you want. You don't have to worry about getting pregnant."

When Christian came to the house, I started to cry. "The doctors sterilized me. I guess you won't want to be my boyfriend anymore."

Christian made the sign for love. "Whatever happens, we'll be together. As soon as you're twenty-one, we'll get married."

In 1938, in spite of being sterilized, I missed my period. Christian became excited. "Now we can get married." He began to look for an apartment.

My mother was out of town helping a sick relative. When she returned, a few months later, she saw my swollen stomach. "How could you do this?"

I blushed. "Please, please, don't be angry. We want a baby so much. I was afraid I'd never have one. Now Christian and I can get married."

"All right, but I want to be sure you have proper care. I want you to go to a gynecologist."

The gynecologist who examined me was very jolly. "Congratulations. The Fuehrer wants every young girl to have a baby."

Then I saw my mother say, "I'm surprised Franziska got pregnant. She's been sterilized."

"Sterilized!" The doctor jumped up and opened the door. "You'll have to leave at once."

Within a few days, I had a letter from the health office. "Fraulein Schwarz is to come to the Women's Hospital for an examination."

I took off my clothes and went into the examining room. The doctor felt my stomach. "Yes, you're pregnant. The pregnancy appears normal. Go into the other room."

In the dressing room, I couldn't find my clothes. I looked in all the drawers and under the seats. They were gone.

I banged on the doctor's door. "Clothes, clothes."

The doctor shook his head. He wrote on a pad. "You stay here. We have to check your urine for three days."

I wrote back. "I don't believe you. I want to go home. I can have my urine checked at home."

The doctor pushed me inside the changing room and locked the door. I looked out the window. I was on the fifth floor, too far to jump. I hid behind the door. When the nurse brought lunch, I escaped and ran toward the stairs. All the nurses ran after me. They caught me and locked me in the room.

For three days, I lay there, biting my nails and screaming. No one came to check my urine or examine me. Then the doctor came in. He pointed to my stomach. His lips moved, saying, "Out."

"What do you mean?"

"Out." He left.

I ran to the window. Even though it was on the fifth floor, I was going to jump. The nurse caught me. She dragged me by the hair into the hall and put me in a room with barred windows. I saw a piece of paper and a pencil on the desk. I wrote a note and then tried the door. It was unlocked. I ran into the hallway. A friend was coming up the steps to see me. I handed her the note. "Please, take it to my mother."

A nurse snatched the note. "You'd better leave," she told my friend. "She's acting a little crazy." I had no time to sign and tell my friend that the doctor was going to take my baby.

All night long I banged on the wall so they would let me out. The nurse shoved me into bed and gave me an injection. I woke up just as the stretcher was being wheeled into the operating room. There was a big tray next to the operating table. My baby is going to be on that tray, I thought, instead of inside me. "No, no," I tried to shout. "Christian, stop them."

When I woke up, I had terrible pains. "Christian, Christian," I moaned. "My uterus feels as though it's burning." I turned to the nurse, "Please, please, let me go to the bathroom."

"No, there are bandages there." Finally, on the third day, the doctor removed the bandage.

Christian didn't know where I was. A few nights earlier, when I hadn't met him in the park, he went to my house.

My mother slammed the door in his face. She was so upset, she took it out on Christian.

Every day, he went to my house, but my mother wouldn't open the door. Finally, he asked his stepmother to find out what had happened to me. She was a friend of my mother.

"Franziska is in the Women's Hospital. They took the baby," my mother told his stepmother. "She keeps calling for Christian."

When I woke up from a nap, I saw Christian standing next to the bed. My face was so white he dropped the flowers he had brought me. "Franziska, I'm sorry they took the baby. But we'll still get married. We can't stop Hitler, but he can't stop us from loving each other."

The nurse handed me a notice when I left the hospital. "You are to return to this hospital within 10 weeks to be sterilized." I crumpled the paper and threw it in the trash can.

When I was well, Christian and I went to the registrar for a marriage license. "I'm sorry," the registrar said. "We have a file on Franziska Schwarz. We can't issue a marriage license until she is sterilized."

I started to cry. "It's hopeless. I won't go. It's too painful. I'll hide in a convent until the war is over. Then we can get married and have children."

"No," Christian said. "The Nazis will find you. They'll take you and do it whether you want it or not. Hitler is winning the war."

My Uncle Karl wrote to the judges for another hearing. He had been trying to help deaf people as much as he could. My mother, my father, and all his brothers went to court. The judges refused to change the order. My uncle's face got very red. "God damn Hitler! How can he do this to a young girl?"

The judge stood up. His face got so red and twisted he looked like the gargoyle in the corner of the church. "Arrest this man. He has slandered the Fuehrer."

Again his brothers tried to get him released. They promised he would join the army and fight for the Fuehrer. The Nazis wouldn't listen. They beheaded Uncle Karl and sent the family the bill for the executioner.

It was a horrible time for me and my family.

"With all the terrible things happening," Christian said, "we should be together. Please get sterilized. I want to get married."

On March 21, 1941, I went to the hospital. After the operation I had a lot of pain.

As soon as I recovered, we were married. In 1943, the apartment in which we were living was bombed. Christian sent me to the country to work for a farmer. The only people who would rent a room to me were other deaf people. Christian came every weekend on his bike from Munich to see me. When the war ended, we had to get permission from the government to return to Munich.

So many houses and apartments had been bombed, we had a hard time finding a place to live. Even after the war, many people were not willing to rent to deaf people. We finally found an attic apartment. To get to our windowless apartment, we had to climb up a ladder. Christian went from one job to another, always seeking better pay. Finally, we were able to afford an apartment with windows. On his last job, he was hired as a supervisor in a factory that employed deaf people. He was lucky; many of our deaf friends had to give up good jobs after the war to the returning war veterans.

After work and on weekends, Christian coached deaf soccer teams. We had lots of friends. I liked to bake strudel and bring it to parties and picnics. Life after the war was better except for one thing: We could not have children. This caused us much pain and regret.

Franziska Schwarz Mikus, who lives in Munich, has been active in promoting arts and crafts among the deaf. Through the years, she has served as secretary to three different organizations for the deaf. Christian Mikus died a few years ago. His death was mourned by the entire deaf community of Germany and Europe. He had become well known for his coaching abilities, and his soccer team had participated in the international deaf games.

6

Regina: Divorce
or Die

Marriages and extramarital intercourse between Jews and citizens of German or related
blood are forbidden.
— Nuremberg Laws, September 15, 1935

As Germany moved into the twentieth century, more and
more Christians and Jews developed family trees with
Christian and Jewish branches. Homes that had previously
kindled Hanukkah candles now trimmed Christmas trees
as Jews intermarried or converted to Christianity. Many
religious leaders and demographers believe that if Germany
had not persecuted the Jews, its so-called Jewish Problem
would have disappeared with assimilation.

In their search for a basis on which to obtain power, the
Nazis revived the theory of "racial purity." They began to
denounce Jews as a corrupting influence on Germany and
blamed them for Germany's losing World War I.

By 1935, they had passed a law forbidding marriages
between Christians and Jews. Christians who were married
to Jews were ordered to divorce their spouses. Those who
refused were sent to concentration camps with their
spouses. Those who could, emigrated.

Under the same law, children of mixed marriages, even

if they had been raised as Christians, were classified as *"mischlinge* (half Jews)." According to the Nazis, these *mischlinge* were a Third Race. Anyone with a Jewish parent or grandparent was classified as a *"mischling*, first degree." Those with two Jewish grandparents and who were raised as Christians became *"mischlinge*, second degree." In many cases, children were not aware that one parent or grandparent was Jewish. They had been raised in the church and knew only Christianity. Many, when they were old enough to marry and applied for a marriage license, found the authorities would not permit them to take a Christian partner.

Mischlinge were excluded from government service and membership in the Nazi party. Any young men who wanted to join the S.S. had to document, through church and city records dating to 1750, that they had no Jewish ancestors. Their fiancées also had to prove their "racial purity."

The laws passed at Nuremberg not only endangered the hundred thousand *mischlinge* but also posed a dilemma for the Nazis. Do you eliminate the "good" German part of the individual along with the "bad" Jewish part?

At first sterilization was urged for *mischlinge*. The idea was dropped when the Nazis realized it would require too many hospital beds and medical personnel. They also noted that attempts to sterilize Jewish girls in Block 10, Auschwitz, had not always been effective. Anxiety grew among the *mischlinge* as Nazi authorities debated their fate.

Because of the need for labor, *mischlinge* were employed in the war production factories. Many were drafted into the army with orders that they not be promoted. However, several did rise to the rank of lieutenant.

In 1944, *mischlinge* serving in the army were pulled out, dishonorably discharged, and sent to labor camps. Many arrived in uniform with their decorations still pinned to their jackets. Civilian *mischlinge* were taken from the factories and transported to labor camps.

Most of Germany's approximately one hundred thousand *mischlinge* survived the war.

Through a ruse, Regina managed to remain married to her Christian husband, Karl. Had Regina and Karl had children, those children would have been subject to the Nazis' racial laws and in danger of being sentenced to death.

———————

I was sixteen when I met Karl. He had come from Berlin to Ellwangen to substitute for our local doctor, who had broken his leg. When he came to the house to treat my mother, we fell in love — at first sight. Although Karl was Christian and eleven years older than I was, my mother did not object to the marriage. "He is a fine man. He will make you a good husband."

All the town officials came to the wedding reception on January 2, 1933, and the fat chief of police waltzed me around and around the hall.

After a brief honeymoon, we set up housekeeping in Berlin. Karl's friends invited us to dinners and to the opera. His mentor, Dr. Schwengl, sent invitations to a ball in our honor on March 3.

A few weeks later, on January 30, 1933, the happiness of our marriage was threatened by Adolf Hitler's being elected chancellor of Germany. Slogans immediately appeared in restaurant and cinema windows, *"Juden und Hunde Verboten* (Jews and dogs not permitted)." We could no longer join friends at a restaurant.

In February the mailman delivered Dr. Schwengl's curt note, "The ball has been canceled." Outside, I heard the crack of the storm troopers' boots as they marched down the street.

In March, Karl came home early. His face was white. "Are you ill?" I asked.

"Regina, give me a *schnapps.*" His hand shook when I handed him the glass. "The S.S. burst into the ward. They grabbed Heinz Cohen and Nathan Goldberg and threw them out the door. The Nazis won't allow any Jewish doctors in the hospitals."

Karl drained his glass. "We have to leave. It can only get worse."

The thought of leaving my parents and my homeland overwhelmed me.

"Where would we go?"

"South Africa, America, anywhere." Karl slammed the glass down. It broke.

On April 1, the Nazis declared a boycott against Jewish-owned stores. Storm troopers, with signs, *"Deutsche! Wehrt Euch! Kauft nicht bei Juden!* (Germans! Beware! Don't buy from the Jews)," blocked the entrances to the stores.

May brought the acrid odor of burning books. The evening of May 10, Karl and I were out for our nightly stroll. Near the University of Berlin, we saw a huge circle of people. Students marched down the library steps, books in one hand, torches in the other. They jeered as they threw the books onto a huge bonfire. In silence, the crowd watched the white pages blacken and crumble. A storm trooper with a megaphone called out the names of the authors of the burning books, "Albert Einstein. Erich Maria Remarque, Goethe, Thomas Mann, Helen Keller, Ring Lardner, Pearl Buck. . . ."

That night, I wrote to my cousins and asked them to send us affidavits to come to America.

They sent them immediately. If Karl and I could obtain visas, we would be safe.

But I was worried about my parents. My mother had written, "Kroll's café now has a sign in the window, '*Juden Unerwuenscht* (Jews Not Wanted).' After forty years, your father can no longer take midmorning coffee with his friends." Since 1774 my family had lived in Ellwangen. Father had been a member of the town council.

In June, I came to visit. As I stepped off the train, I nodded at a former neighbor. He turned his head and darted into an alley. By the time I reached home, he had chalked a message over the doorway of my house, "Stop Race Defilement." As I rubbed off the sign with my sleeve, I remembered when my younger sister was born. The village band had marched up the hill to trumpet a welcome.

The months passed. On January 2, 1934, our first anniversary, Karl came home with red roses and champagne. "For Regina, my most beautiful bride." Though we tried to joke and be festive over my dinner of roast goose with apple and chestnut stuffing, our forks stayed next to our plates. The front pages of *Der Stuermer*, the Nazi newspaper, had carried a picture of a Christian doctor, whose office was next to Karl's, and his Jewish girlfriend. The headline read, "Doctor Arrested for 'Race Defilement.'"

As I put a sacher torte, Karl's favorite dessert, on the table, he could no longer hold back his fury. "The Nazis are refusing exit permits to Christian doctors."

I stared at the bubbles in my champagne glass. "If we can't get out, then for the sake of your career, your very life, we'll have to divorce." My face flushed. Though I was only seventeen, I sometimes felt wiser than Karl. "If we divorce, the Nazis will feel you are loyal to the regime. They'll let you go to London to attend the medical conference. We can meet in Southampton and take the boat to America." I looked at the silver candlesticks that had been passed down from my grandmother. "It's our only chance for a family, a normal life."

He clasped my wrist and kissed my hand. "Regina, I married you forever. Look, I'm treating some Nazi officials. I can bribe them."

"No," I said. "At the very least, you'll lose your hospital privileges. At the worst, I'll never see you again."

"Not a divorce. A separation. Perhaps things will get better. But where will you go? You can't go back to your parents."

"I'll get a room in a boarding house. We'll meet at my cousin's house on Sundays." I didn't want to tell Karl how scared I was. The thought of being separated from him, of being on my own, was frightening.

As the Nazi spy network grew, our secret meetings became more and more dangerous. By July 1934, I knew I had to stop seeing Karl at my cousin's house. Karl and I arranged to meet in Bad Godesberg. It could be our last meeting. Karl could not continue to practice medicine and remain married to a Jew. But he was still reluctant to have me file divorce papers. "It doesn't seem right . . ." He stopped in midsentence, silenced by the sound of an approaching motorcade. We peered over the balcony. The terrace and the driveway of the hotel next door were illuminated by lighted torches. Six hundred young men wearing the uniform of the Nazi Youth Labor Corps stood at attention, their arms thrust upward in the Nazi salute. The long line of Mercedes cars stopped. A chauffeur opened the door of the open-topped car.

Six hundred flares burst into a flaming swastika as Adolf Hitler stepped onto the pavement. The band broke into a march and the voices of six hundred young men resounded across the valley. *"Sieg Heil, Sieg Heil, Sieg Heil,"* they shouted, welcoming their leader.

Karl and I clung to one another, terrified. "You're right," he whispered. "There is no other solution."

The next day, I returned to Berlin and filed for a divorce.

For a country that urged the dissolution of marriages between Christians and Jews, the courts moved slowly. Each morning I searched the mailbox for the notice to appear at the divorce hearing. I grew more apprehensive in September 1935, with the passage of the Nuremberg Laws. The laws deprived Jews of their citizenship. Equally terrifying was the law that forbade marriages between Jews and Christians. Anyone who disobeyed the Nuremberg Laws would be punished by "hard labor" — imprisonment.

But the Nuremberg Laws brought me a personal blessing. Two days after their passage, I was called for a hearing. The judge asked only one question, "Are you Jewish?"
"Yes."
"Divorce granted."

My cousins had sent us affidavits. All we needed were visas.

Wearing a heavy black veil, I walked toward the American Embassy. A line of Germans seeking visas stretched around the embassy and across the street. "Please, I have an appointment," I said, walking past men with their hats pulled down over their foreheads and other women with veils. I could feel the envy as the crowd moved aside. Karl sat at the far end of the waiting room, his face hidden behind a newspaper. I took a seat on the other side. Some of the women left the consul's office crying.

I heard my name, "Regina Hauptmann."

Karl followed a few minutes later. The consul shook his head when he heard that we were divorced. "I'm sorry, but it's against American policy to issue visas to divorced women." He stood up to dismiss me.

"The minute we are out of Germany, we'll remarry," Karl protested.

The consul looked at the stacks of applications on his desk. "I'm sorry. I can't make an exception for a divorced woman. Besides, she's a minor. How will she support herself if you can't get out?"

"I've already had two thousand dollars deposited in each of our names in New York. I'm a doctor. I can make a living anywhere."

I berated myself. Why hadn't I found out about visas for divorced women? But if I hadn't gotten the divorce, Karl would be in prison.

Karl bristled. "For God's sake, the Nazis forced us to get a divorce. We love each other. We simply want to live together as man and wife, to raise a family. Is this too simple a request to ask of a great country like America?"

I wept.

"How can I be sure you're not lying? People are swearing to anything to get out of Germany."

Karl walked over to his desk. "Six years ago, I took an oath as a doctor. Next to my marriage vows, it is the most precious oath that I shall ever take." He raised his right hand. "On my Hippocratic oath, I swear to you that at the first possible moment, we shall remarry." Karl told him our plans. "I have an invitation to deliver a lecture in England. Since I proved my loyalty by divorcing my wife, the Nazis will let me go. When Regina reaches Le Havre, France, she'll telegraph me in London and tell me which ship to board. I'll meet her ship in Southampton."

"All right, doctor, but before I can grant your wife a visa, she will have to send me a letter telling me how you mistreated her. The more inhuman your husband seems, madam, the easier it will be for me to grant the visa." He lifted his rubber stamp as he reached for Karl's passport.

"No," I screamed, snatching the passport from his hands. "That's a death sentence. Give me his visa on a separate piece of paper. I'll smuggle it into England."

At the boarding house, I ripped open the lining of my skirt and sewed Karl's visa inside the hem. Then I spread my application on the table. What terrible things could I say about my kind, loving husband? I couldn't imagine a man hurting his wife. Then I remembered a movie I had seen about a man who beat his wife. Swiftly, I wrote down the scenario of the script.

The morning the postman delivered my visa, I took a taxi to the train station. During the long ride to the French border, I wondered if our dreams would ever be fulfilled. Would Karl be allowed to attend the conference, or would I find myself alone in a strange country? I knew a little English, but I had no trade, only a few lessons in typing and German shorthand. When I was growing up, Germans still believed in "*Kirche, Kuche, und Kinder* (church, kitchen, and children)." Proper young ladies studied embroidery and the piano to prepare them for life.

The train stopped on the German side of the border.

"Everyone off." The German guard glared at the "*J*" for Jew stamped on my passport. "Inside the house," he snapped.

I was led into a small room. A huge woman, at least six feet tall with legs as solid as an elephant's, glared at me. "Take off all your clothes."

I stood there shivering, humiliated as her rough hands searched every part of my body for hidden diamonds.

"Unfasten your braids," she ordered, tugging at my hair.

I pulled out the tortoiseshell hairpin. My blonde hair flowed down my back. The border was so close. Would she search the hem of my skirt and discover Karl's visa? If she did . . .

She rubbed her fingers through my scalp seeking rubies. With a yank on my hair, she grunted, "Open your mouth, wide." Her fingers stretched the ends of my lips as she peered behind my gums. She shoved me against the wall. "Get dressed."

When I reached Cherbourg, France, I sent a telegram to

Karl, who was in London. "Sailing on the *Île de France.* Ship docks Southampton Tuesday."

In London, Karl kept inquiring at the concierge's desk for the telegram that never arrived. Had something gone wrong? Was I still in Germany? A sixth sense made him grab a train to Southampton. Whatever ship was sailing to America would be the ship I was on, he reasoned. But when he arrived in Southampton, it was dark. Three ocean liners were preparing to sail for America. He ran aboard the first ship. There was no Regina Hauptmann on the manifest. He heard the blast of the *Île de France's* horn. He ran off the first ship and up the gangplank of the *Île de France* moments before the sailors hauled it aboard. It was midnight.

"The purser's office is closed," the deck officer told him. "You'll have to wait until morning to check the passenger list."

Karl could not sleep. What if I were not aboard? What if I had been detained at the border? What would he do in New York without a visa?

That evening, I had stood at the ship's rail watching the passengers board at Southampton. Had the Gestapo discovered our plans and seized him? Would I ever see him again? I heard the call, "All aboard. All ashore that's going ashore." There was no one on the dock. I walked to my cabin and burst into tears.

The next morning, my face swollen from crying, I walked into the dining room. Perhaps Karl had taken one of the other ships in the harbor. I had to find the captain, have him cable them. My eyes blurred from the tears I could not stop. I stood at the dining room entrance. The chatter of excited voyagers filled the room. My eyes had trouble focusing on the numbers at each table. Where was number 17? How could I live without Karl? Had I signed his death warrant? I stumbled past the tables. Someone stood up and reached out to stop me.

I blindly pushed his arm aside.

"It's all right, *Liebchen*," Karl said, taking me in his arms. "I'm here."

I was full of apprehension as we sailed into New York harbor. Would Karl's credentials be sufficient for him to practice medicine? How would the medical community receive a specialist from abroad?

Suddenly, I caught my breath. Before us rose the Statue of Liberty, its torch held high. As a schoolgirl studying English, I had memorized the sonnet beneath it:

Give me your tired, your poor,
Your huddled masses yearning to breathe free,
The wretched refuse of your teeming shore,
Send these, the homeless, tempest-tossed to me:
I lift my lamp beside the golden door.

Reassured, I watched as the ship passed Ellis Island, as it sailed up the Hudson River. The skyline of Manhattan was a maze of skyscrapers, with the Empire State building towering over them.

At last the ship docked. Crowds waited at the gangplank for the passengers to disembark.

I watched the immigration official, a short man with pinched nostrils, come aboard. His badge and every button on his uniform reflected the sun.

He examined my passport and visa carefully. "Everything is in order. You may leave the ship." I handed him the separate visa for Karl.

The official turned it over, examining both sides. He felt the paper and put on his glasses to peer at the ink. With a snort, he handed it back. "This is a fake. Your husband will have to return to Germany."

Karl could scarcely speak. "But it's official. It would have been suicidal to have my visa stamped in my passport. Don't you understand what's happening in Germany?"

The customs official refused to believe Karl had a valid visa. He ordered the captain to take him back to Germany.

I stared at this arrogant minor official. Didn't he know he was giving Karl a death sentence?

Karl's face turned gray, and he was unable to speak. He stood at the rail, looking at the black waters of the river. The ship was to sail in a few hours.

My cousins, who had been waiting at the foot of the gangplank, came aboard. "This is outrageous," my cousin Jonah said. "I'll call my congressman. He'll straighten it out."

An hour later, the congressman's assistant boarded the ship. He had checked with the State Department. The visa was valid. The immigration official still refused to believe him.

The congressman's assistant ran down the gangplank. "I'll be right back."

I watched the ship take on provisions for the return voyage.

An hour later, the head of the Bureau of Immigration

boarded the ship. "The passport is valid," he said. "Welcome to America, Doctor."

Like all foreign doctors who came to America, Karl Hauptmann (a pseudonym to protect his privacy) had to study for the American medical boards before he could practice in New York State. When America entered the war, he enlisted in the army and was assigned to Walter Reed Hospital. After the war, he became a professor at a medical school and trained some of America's outstanding internists. The Hauptmanns' three children were born in the United States.

7

No Blacks
Allowed

The mulatto children came about through rape or the white mother was a whore. In both cases, there is not the slightest moral duty regarding these offspring of a foreign race.
— Adolf Hitler

After World War I, Allied troops occupied the Rhineland. The French sent in units from Morocco, Tunisia, Algeria, the Cameroons, and Senegal. They were either black or Arab. The presence of these dark-skinned soldiers was bitterly resented by the Germans. Even before Hitler, Germans were very color-conscious. Though Germany had had colonies in Africa prior to World War I, there were taboos against Germans marrying black women. The introduction of black troops after World War I became known as the "Black Disgrace." Vicious cartoons condemning the "*neger*" circulated in the newspapers.

Some of the black soldiers married German women and had families. Others fathered illegitimate children. All of the children became known as the "Rhineland Bastards."

In *Mein Kampf*, Hitler wrote that he would eliminate all traces of this "insult" (half-black–half-German children) to the German nation.

Though black entertainers were popular in Germany before Hitler came to power, they were boycotted when the Nazis took over. A book entitled *Degenerate Music: An Accounting* was published in 1938. The cover shows a black musician with a Jewish star in his lapel. Hitler's hatred of blacks extended to black athletes. When Jesse Owens, the American track star, won three gold medals at the 1936 Olympics in Berlin, Hitler refused to be present when the medals were presented.

There were no laws on the books specifying actions against blacks, but the Nazis set up a secret group, Commission Number 3, whose mission was to arrange for the sterilization of the so-called Rhineland Bastards. In 1937, local authorities were asked to submit documents on all known persons in this insulting category.

The action was taken under the "Law for the Prevention of Offspring with Hereditary Defects" issued in 1933.

Three commissions were to certify which children were "Rhineland Bastards." Anthropologists from universities served as advisors to these three-member commissions. Professor Eugen Fischer of the Kaiser Wilhelm Institute was among them. Children were removed from homes and schools or picked up off the street and taken before the commission. They had no representation. Once the decision was handed down, the children were taken directly to the hospital and sterilized. Approximately four hundred were sterilized.

Though there were relatively few blacks in Germany, Hitler discriminated between black and white prisoners of war. Black soldiers captured during World War II were separated from their units and shot.

When the Germans tried to remove a black lieutenant

from Martinique from his French comrades, his superior officer objected. "He is not black," the colonel explained to the Germans. "He is an officer."

Instead of shooting him, the Germans placed the man in a prisoner of war camp according to the Geneva conventions. The lieutenant knew he was one of the lucky ones. A short time later, he managed to escape.

If Hitler had been successful in Africa, large numbers of black troops would have been shot.

Historians are just beginning to examine the Nazi files on blacks. Much of the information has yet to be obtained and made available to the public. To date, the few existent publications are available only in German.

PART IV
Mind Control

8

Wolfgang: Flight from Censorship

Propaganda does not have to state the truth
objectively . . . but must serve its own interests uninterruptedly.

— Adolf Hitler

Through mind control, both in education and by exposure
to the arts, Hitler planned to indoctrinate a new generation
of Germans. Docile, obedient, and physically strong,
young men would be inspired to fight for him. Young girls
would be eager to bear soldiers for his future armies.

By selective use of various forms of art, Hitler introduced his racial theories to a whole generation. Textbooks
were rewritten to show the Jew as ugly and unscrupulous.
Teachers unwilling to teach the new curriculum were dis-
missed. All authors had to submit books for approval before they could be published. No views contrary to Hitler's
were printed in the press. Only films that represented the
Nazi viewpoint were shown, and the concert halls were
forbidden to present the music of Jewish and modern com-
posers. Each group of artists had to be members of a Nazi
organization for the arts in order to obtain work.

The work, of course, was to be executed according to
the Nazi definition of art, which meant pictures of muscle-

bulging soldiers, bosomy mothers, and placid country landscapes. In the world of music, it meant military marches in addition to Wagner, Beethoven, Bach, and Brahms.

The Nazis quickly banned all foreign publications as well as books by Jewish writers and liberals. As Regina's story told, on the night of May 10, 1933, huge bonfires were kindled throughout Germany to burn the banned books. Storm troopers and university students raided library shelves and private homes for books to throw into the flames. At the University of Berlin, twenty thousand books were destroyed. The Minister of Propaganda, Joseph Goebbels, commended the destruction, declaring, "From these ashes will arise the phoenix of a new spirit. . . . The past is lying in flames. The future will arise from the flames within our own hearts. . . ."

At press conferences, newspapermen were told what to write. Reporters were not allowed to ask questions. The assault on the senses was everywhere. Posters were plastered on the walls of subways, kiosks, railroad stations, and sides of buildings. Such slogans as "The Jews Are Our Misfortune" encouraged anti-Semitism. One, with a picture of a blond-haired youngster in the foreground and Hitler in the background, glorified Hitler Youth.

Hitler, who had been refused admission to an art school as a youth, declared that his taste would decide what was art. In July 1937, when he presided at the opening of the House of German Art in Munich, he proclaimed, "The people in passing through these galleries will recognize in me its own spokesman and counselor . . . and gladly express its agreement with this purification of art."

In his attempt to purify art, Hitler ordered the removal of paintings by Cezanne, Gauguin, Matisse, Van Gogh, and other great impressionists from German museums. The work of expressionists and abstract artists as well as of Jews was banned and confiscated. Many pieces of their art were sold outside Germany or were destroyed. Before this took place, an exhibit of "degenerate" art was held in Munich in an attempt to prove the worthlessness of the banned art. So many art lovers made a special trip to Munich to see the exhibit that Goebbels soon canceled it.

Six months after Hitler became chancellor, fifty thousand people from the various arts had left Germany. Some left because they were married to Jews. Others knew that the restriction of artists was only the beginning of a reign of terror.

Those who remained in Germany tried to protest by writing or speaking in "slave language" or "coded" speech. Sooner or later they were either forced to be silent or, like Carl von Ossietzky, an editor and a winner of the Nobel Peace Prize, were sent to concentration camps. In the camps, a few secretly managed to produce and hide drawings. Most died from the brutal treatment in the camps.

Many artists went underground by working in defense industries and setting aside their art for the duration of the war. They are known as the German "lost generation" of artists. Their inability to continue halted their artistic development.

Their contemporaries who managed to emigrate to America continued to work as artists and writers. Many became successful. Wolfgang Behl, who dreamed of becoming a sculptor, was one of the artists who had to flee from Germany in order to practice his art.

———•———

My name is Wolfgang Behl and I couldn't believe the letter my classmates at the Kaiser Friedrich High School were passing out. It was dated September 22, 1935.

> 1. Members of the class are to have no friendly relations with Jews.
> 2. Don't even say hello to them.
> 3. Jews are to sit apart from the rest of the class.
> 4. No German is to work together with Jews on school work.
> 5. Jews will not participate in hikes and excursions or any extracurricular activities.

It was signed by six members of the class who were always strutting around in Hitler Youth uniforms: Grimm, Schultze, Weinaug, Scharnetky, Bosse, and Mueller-Guellich. Five non–party members added their signatures: Langenheim, Hoffmann, Schubert, Speckin, and Rost.

I was shocked. Half of the class was Jewish, and many of my parents' friends were Jewish. For years, my father had been Superintendent of Theater in Berlin. We went to opening night performances, and Father had the wonderful job of deciding which plays and cabaret acts could be produced. Since Jews were active in the theater, as well as in literature and music and art, they were often in our house. Though we were Lutherans, we judged a person by his or her talents and character, not by religion. At fourteen, I had already decided I wanted to be a sculptor.

Now, as I stood at my desk, I grew angrier and angrier as I reread the letter. I turned around and slammed it on Schultze's desk. "Who in hell do you think you are?" Everyone knew that the Jewish students were the best in the class.

Schultze stood up. Though he was only fifteen, he was a good six inches taller than I. "Shut up, you 'white' Jew." He and his friends had been furious when I had refused to join the Hitler Youth. "You're not a real German," he said, pushing me to the floor.

I jumped up and punched him in the nose. When he tried to hit back, I ducked and jabbed him in the stomach. He fell down. Then Weinaug jumped me. I dug my elbow in his groin. He let go and I dashed out of the room and hightailed it for home. I had picked a fight with the son of a party leader. I was in real trouble.

As soon as I blurted out my story, Mother took out my rucksack. "What you did was right, but the police will be here any minute. You've got to leave Berlin."

Within an hour I was on a train to the country. Friends of my parents took me in, and I kept busy making wood carvings. A few months later, Father wrote, "It's safe to come back. The S.S. is busy with bigger fish. Since you can't return to high school, I've arranged for you to study secretly at the Academy of Fine Arts. Otto Hitzberger is willing to take you into his studio as an unregistered student."

Otto Hitzberger was a wonderful teacher and storyteller. As he worked on a wood carving of Christ on the Cross, he enlivened my lessons with tales of hunting seals in the Arctic and life as a German colonist in Africa. Since I was not registered, I didn't have to join the Nazis' Student Bund, although anyone registered at the school had to join the Bund. Otherwise, they couldn't go to art school. It was the same thing for those enrolled in the university or music school.

On weekends while the other students marched in Nazi parades, I went sailing on Lake Wannsee. I was joined by my Jewish friends and one non-Jewish friend. The Jewish students had been kicked out of high school because of their religion, and most were trying to get visas to leave Germany.

Whenever I walked to school, my eyes were constantly assaulted by Nazi propaganda posters. The colorful drawings were plastered on buildings, billboards, and newsstands. Pictures of blonde, bosomy young women and muscular soldiers exhorted everyone either to breed or to fight for Hitler. One of the posters showed Jews as evil, greedy hunchbacks.

For me, the art school became an island of sanity in the midst of insanity. Somehow, the professors were left alone to produce whatever kind of art they pleased. Then, in 1937, the Nazis stripped the German museums of all so-called degenerate art. Pictures and sculptures by German expressionists, the Dutch painter Van Gogh, and all Jewish painters vanished from the gallery walls. Though he was not Jewish, Otto Hitzberger's "Christ on the Cross" was confiscated. Together, we sat in the studio, mourning the Nazis' barbarism. As a warning on what not to paint, the Nazis held an exhibition of the seized paintings in Munich. The exhibition was called *"Entartige Kunst* (Degenerate

Art)." Like thousands of others, I went to Munich to say goodbye to the pictures and sculptures I had admired.

I wanted desperately to leave Germany, but we had very little money. Finally, on November 10, 1938, I realized I had to get out.

I had stayed up late the night before, working on a wood carving. Since my parents were on vacation, I didn't bother to turn on a radio. Early the next morning, I left the apartment. As I came out of the building, an ominous silence hung over the Kurfurstendam, the most fashionable street in Berlin. People stood in clusters, silent. I stared at the shops owned by Jews. The windows had been shattered and broken glass covered the sidewalks; the shops were empty of goods. I crossed to the other side of the Kurfurstendam and gaped at the gutted, still smouldering, synagogue.

"What happened?" I asked a man who stood nearby.

He shook his head and walked away.

I bought a newspaper and read the headlines: "Spontaneous Riots Sweep Germany," "Jews Get What They Deserve."

As I read, the details of the nationwide action against Jews seemed unreal. The Nazis had rounded up thousands of Jewish men in addition to destroying synagogues and shops.

"My God," I thought, "our friends are in danger!" I ran home and began to call my parents' Jewish friends. "This is Wolfgang. Come to our apartment. My parents aren't home, but you'll be safe here." I hung up and dialed a former classmate.

His mother started to cry. "He was arrested last night! I don't know why."

That afternoon, fourteen friends crowded into our apartment. I went out into the street and bought food.

"Look, I'll check your apartments every day. When it's safe, you can leave." A few days later, everything had died down. Our friends returned to their homes.

"Crystal Night" was a warning — to Jews and to anyone else who would not go along with the Nazis. With my big mouth, I had to escape. As soon as it was warm enough, I would paddle my kayak across the Baltic Sea to Norway. My parents and I agreed I should wait until May.

In April, I received a letter that read, "Wolfgang Behl is to report for a physical examination prior to induction into the army. Heil Hitler." There was no escape. I was strong and muscular from days spent rowing and canoeing.

As I stood in the school gym with three hundred other young men, I looked like the perfect Aryan: blue eyed and blond haired. I didn't believe in war. If I passed, I would be forced to fight for a ruler I hated. I would also lose my passport. As soon as they were inducted, soldiers had to turn in their passports. Hitler didn't want anyone escaping to another country. From the eye doctor, I went to the ear doctor, from the ear doctor to someone who checked for flat feet. Finally, I came to the last doctor. He sat like a king on a dais. He looked me over carefully. "What is your occupation?"

"Student of sculpture," I said, miserable over the prospect of being in the army.

"Do ten knee bends."

I began the exercise.

"Stop. There's something wrong. Come up on the platform." He held his stethoscope over my heart. He shook his head. "Too bad. Heart condition. Sorry, you're not fit for service." He stamped my papers: "Unfit for draft. Physical disability."

I couldn't believe my luck. The only other person excused from the service was a hunchback. I ran outside. Then I stopped. With a heart condition, I shouldn't be exerting myself. When my mother heard the news, she was happy but alarmed. "We have to see our own doctor right away."

Dr. B. had treated our family for years. He listened to my heart. "The doctor's crazy, Wolfgang. You're as healthy as an ox. But that's our secret."

"As soon as I can borrow the money, you're leaving," my father said. "There's no sense risking a second examination." He also had to find someone who would give me an affidavit to guarantee the American government that the signer would be financially responsible for me.

Father wrote to a distant cousin in New York. "Wolfgang would like to visit America and meet his American cousin."

Since Cousin Hans had an eligible daughter, he sent an affidavit and a letter inviting me to come to New York. A Jewish friend gave my father the money for my trip. His son and I were to leave Berlin on the same train. As we sat in the second-class car anxiously waiting for our eleven P.M. departure, we saw train after train filled with troops heading east. I began to sweat. What if a guard didn't believe my papers and pulled me off the train before it crossed the border? Finally, the train started. I grew nervous each time it stopped and the German police inspected our visas.

Several hours later, we stopped at the Dutch border. Each side was heavily guarded. After a thorough inspection, the train crossed the frontier into Holland. Immediately, I smelled the sweet air of freedom.

In July, Cousin Hans met me on Ellis Island. "Heil Hitler," he said, raising his arm in the Nazi salute.

His daughter, a short blonde-haired girl, seemed embarrassed.

"Ach, Germany," he said, as he drove toward his house on Staten Island. "The greatest country in the world. I belong to the German American Bund," he said proudly. "I contribute to the Fatherland."

"Do you know what is happening there? What they're doing to Jews and people who disagree with them?" I asked in disbelief. It was dark, and I could see the lights of the skyscrapers outlining Manhattan.

"Jews? Who cares about Jews. All I know, Germany is proud again."

We stopped at a stone house. Lace doilies covered the arms of the couch, and a picture of Adolf Hitler sat on top of the upright piano.

"So, how long are you here?" he asked as he filled a stein with beer.

"Permanently. I want to continue my education. There wasn't too much opportunity for a sculptor in Germany. You could only work on certain kinds of sculpture."

"A strong boy like you should fight for the Fuehrer."

That night, I couldn't sleep. I had gone from Nazism to Nazism. Cousin Hans had signed an affidavit for me. How long could I hold my tongue?

For six weeks, I tried politely but firmly to tell him what

was happening in Germany. One morning, before I could take a sip of coffee, he pointed his finger at me. "You're a draft dodger, that's what you are. And I won't support anyone who doesn't support the Fuehrer."

I had to stall until I could make some arrangements. "But it's difficult to get return passage. Besides, I don't have any money for a ticket."

"I'll give you ten dollars a week for four weeks. After that, I'll revoke your affidavit. The government will ship you back to Germany. Heil Hitler." He left for work.

His daughter tried to be helpful. "Why don't you go to the Christian Relief Agency? Maybe they can help you."

I had already talked with some friends who had fled to New York a few years earlier. After I rented a room in Brooklyn Heights, I took the subway to the American Academy of Art.

"Do you want a job?" a professor asked. "We need someone to make paper masks for the Ballet Russe de Monte Carlo."

"You bet." Not only did I need the money, but I would be with other artists.

That evening, I went to the Christian Relief Service. "Here's a list of people who might help. But an awful lot of people have approached them. Good luck," the receptionist said.

There were over a hundred names on the list. Each day I knocked on at least one door. But no one wanted to take a chance on a struggling art student. Germany had just invaded Poland. I couldn't return to Germany. What could I do? Finally, someone gave me the name of George Gordon Battle, a prominent lawyer. He was on the phone when his secretary ushered me into his corner office. I sat quietly in the chair and stared at the view of the bay from the skyscraper. His desk, which was at least ten feet long, was covered with piles of papers. His second telephone rang. "Just a minute," he said to the person on the line. He looked at me. "What can I do for you?"

"My name is Wolfgang Behl. I'm an art student. I want to stay in this country, and I need someone to sign an affidavit for me. I'll work very hard, and I won't become a responsibility. I'm very talented," I added, thinking how ridiculous my recitation sounded. I had said it so often, I had it down to thirty seconds.

Mr. Battle nodded. "Leave your address with my secretary. We'll be in touch."

I walked out of there, devastated. Visions of returning to Germany made it hard for me to concentrate as I walked toward the subway. I was alone and without friends. What could I do?

The next morning, someone banged on the door. "Telegram for Wolfgang Behl."

I opened it. It was from George Gordon Battle and I read, "COME TO MY OFFICE AT TEN A.M. AND I'LL ARRANGE FOR AN AFFIDAVIT."

My parents were overjoyed when I wrote to them. Father wrote to a member of the Academy of Art who had emigrated to the United States. The man arranged for the Institute of International Education to give me a fellowship to the Rhode Island School of Design. As I stepped off the train in Providence, Rhode Island, I was at last free to become a sculptor.

*

For many years Wolfgang Behl taught sculpture at the University of Hartford Art School. He retired as professor emeritus. He and his wife, Lula Marie, spend their summers in Hartford and their winters in Portugal. Their daughter, Elizabeth, is a hydrogeologist. After the war, his father served as an expert witness at the Nuremberg Trials.

9

Grete: Dissenters Will
Be Prosecuted

> Every attempt to impose another political
> opinion or even to entertain one will be
> treated as a symptom of a sickness endanger-
> ing the healthy unity of the indivisible organ-
> ism of the *Volk* [people], and eradicated
> without regard to the subjective intentions of
> its carrier.
> — S.S. Internal Report

"One people, one country, one leader" was the rallying cry
of the Nazi party. All forms of opposition to Adolf Hitler
were to be ruthlessly destroyed. Under the theory of
"gleichschaltung (complete conformity)," everyone had to
think alike in Nazi Germany.

In his drive to control everyone's thinking, Hitler created
an organization of Nazi groups that involved almost every
German. They included sports groups, Hitler Youth
groups, organizations for businessmen, factory workers,
artists, the deaf, women, and others. Membership in the
Nazi Student Bund was required for anyone who wanted
to attend the university. "Heil Hitler" meant more than a
salute; it meant complete surrender to mind control.

How was Hitler able to establish this uniformity as soon
as he came to power in 1933? Within a short time after he
became chancellor, he persuaded the legislators to pass the

Enabling Act, which gave Hitler the right to rule by decree. He could impose any law that he saw fit. Not only the Nazis voted to give him this power. The Social Democrats (SPD), Hitler's opponents, cast their ballots in favor of the Enabling Act. Why? In times of stress, people are often stampeded into believing that the short-term deprivation of civil rights is for the good of the country, viewing the lapse of personal freedom as only temporary. The Social Democrats feared the Communists and felt that Hitler was at least better than Communism. Similarly, the Communists had supported Hitler against the SPD. After the passage of the Enabling Act, Hitler immediately outlawed all other political parties, including the SPD.

To enforce obedience to the Nazi party, members of other parties were arrested and sent to concentration camps. Liberal newspapers were silenced. Writers, editors, artists, and actors who criticized the party were murdered or sent to concentration camps. Children were taught in school to report any conversations by their parents that were against the Nazis. Block leaders spied on their neighbors' activities. People were afraid to talk to one another on the street. Any remark could be considered treason. In 1943, a brilliant young pianist, Karl Robert Kreiten, casually remarked to one of his mother's friends, "Hitler is losing the war." The woman reported him to the Gestapo. As the young man was about to begin a concert, he was arrested. A few days later, Karl Robert Kreiten was beheaded for treason.

Despite the danger, there continued to be pockets of resistance. Underground networks developed and many of the groups met under the cover of sports clubs that were not part of the Nazi structure. Social Democrats, Communists, and other groups worked to smuggle Jews and others in danger out of the country. They distributed anti-Nazi literature. It was dangerous because persons known to have been members of outlawed political parties were under surveillance. In the middle of the night, the Gestapo would wake them and search their apartments. Some were imprisoned either on suspicion or because of actual evidence.

With the constant surveillance by the Gestapo and neighbors who were members of the Nazi party, resistance in Germany became more and more difficult.

The most widely known act of resistance was the Generals' Plot to assassinate Hitler. In 1944, with the connivance of other generals who were disillusioned with Hitler, Claus von Stauffenberg placed a suitcase containing a bomb against a table next to Hitler. A colonel accidentally kicked the suitcase away from the table. When the bomb exploded, it set Hitler's hair on fire and burned his right leg. Four men died, six people were wounded, but Hitler survived. Von Stauffenberg had excused himself to make a telephone call just before the bomb went off. When he heard the explosion and saw the building collapse, he assumed the assassination was successful. He was wrong. He and his associates were immediately arrested and executed. Thousands were rounded up, tried, and executed in a terrible revenge.

By the end of the war, the German people had learned a cruel lesson: once you give up your rights to think and to question and to pass your own laws, it is difficult to regain those rights.

Grete Hamacher's father, a Social Democrat, was known for his anti-Nazi feelings. The moment the Nazis attained power, the whole family was under constant surveillance.

———•———

"It's better you don't know where I'm sleeping," my father, Heinrich Hamacher, whispered to my mother. "Then the Nazis can't force you to tell them anything."

His rucksack lay on the chair. Father bent down to kiss me. "Goodbye, Grete, my little sparrow, listen to your mother." He lifted the rucksack onto his shoulders and opened the door. I heard the steps creak as he tiptoed down the three flights to the courtyard. He had to be very careful. The innkeeper who owned our apartment had threatened to tell the Nazis about Father's activities.

At six I was used to my father's being away overnight and on weekends. Usually, he bounced down the stairs and slammed the door as he left. As secretary of the Social Democratic party, he had frequently traveled from Cologne to cities all over Germany. Now, he slept at a different house each night to hide from the Nazis. After they came to power in 1933, the Nazis had outlawed all other political parties. Trucks filled with storm troopers raced through the streets rounding up Communist and Socialist leaders to send them to concentration camps.

My father was known as a free thinker. As a young man, he had left the Catholic church because the church had supported the army in World War I. It had even blessed German weapons. After the war, he joined the Communist party. By 1924, he was disillusioned with the Communists. They refused to let their followers ask any questions about their policies. He became active in the Social Democratic party, the SPD. By 1931, he was chief secretary of the SPD in the Cologne area.

Now, in 1933, two years later, the storm troopers were trying to find him and put him in prison as a "political unreliable." They suspected him of distributing flyers that urged people to resist the Nazis. At least once a week I heard the sharp slap of boots as the Gestapo ran up the steps to inspect our attic apartment. The men from the Gestapo threw everything out of Mother's neatly kept closets and overturned the chests. They ripped the sheets off the beds. They examined every piece of paper, including my first grade homework.

Since Father was unable to work, Mother took in sewing. In those days, nothing was wasted. Her golden fingers took torn dresses and turned them into blouses and underwear. Our dwelling lay outside the working-class Cologne suburb called Stammheim. A group of five houses faced the Rhine River. Behind the houses, each family had its own garden and chickens. In March, when the green tips of the daffodils began to peek through the soil, we planted potatoes, onions, and beets. I hated having to pull the weeds, so I loved the times when it rained. I could sit by the window overlooking the Rhine and read.

As soon as the weather was warm enough for boating, Mother and I went to the Workers' Sports Club. Father and his four brothers were good swimmers. With the other members of the Workers' Gymnastics and Sports Committee, he had built a boathouse on the Rhine. The river front was lined with floats built by various clubs. My parents took me paddle boating. I loved waving to the freighters and ships that sailed toward Cologne. It was here, on a lovely June afternoon, that Uncle Willie came to fetch us.

"Hein was taken last night," he said as he reached down to tie up our boat.

My blonde, rosy-cheeked mother turned white. "Where?"

"To Friesland. The concentration camp at Esterwegen." Uncle Willie helped us out of the boat. "The authorities have forbidden anyone to get in touch with him."

"But that's swampland! Why there?"

"To dig peat for fuel and fertilizer. What cheaper labor than prisoners?" Uncle Willie lifted me onto his shoulders to carry me home. Mother was too upset to talk.

For six months, we heard nothing about Father. At the end of November, we received a letter from Esterwegen. "Because I was wounded in World War I, I will be released in a few days."

"I'll meet his train at the station and bring him home on the streetcar," Mother told me. "Wait for us at the streetcar stop."

I stood beside the path waiting for them to come. Mother got off the streetcar, but where was Father? The only other person leaving the car was a very thin man with a beard. The man's skin was dark, like that of someone used to working in the sun.

"Grete, my little sparrow," the man said, bending down and taking me in his arms. I had not recognized my own father, he had changed so.

We climbed the steps to the apartment. "Things will be all right now that I'm home," Father said. "I'll go to the factory and get my old job back. There's lots of work now that Hitler's building trucks and tanks."

115

"I'm sorry, Hein," the foreman said. "I need you, but I can't hire you. Your identity papers are stamped 'DON'T HIRE.' Maybe you should join the Nazi party, just to get work."

"They're trying to squeeze the life's blood out of me," he raged when he came home. He banged his fist on the wall. "But I still won't join their damn party."

"No," Mother said quietly. "I'll take in more sewing and laundry. We'll plant more food."

Father was not one to be idle. Illegally, he left Germany to attend conferences and meet with other socialist leaders. Mother must have known what he was doing, because I could hear them whispering at night. After the war, I found he had helped to smuggle refugees across the border. Once I woke up in the middle of the night to find him burning papers in the fireplace.

By 1935, I had grown so much that the sleeves of my winter coat reached only to my elbows. A neighbor who saw me shivering as I walked home from school got me a secondhand coat through the Nazi welfare organization. Though Mother worked as hard as she could, we would have gone hungry many times if my grandparents and uncles and aunts hadn't brought us money to pay the rent and buy staples. How I loved it when Grandfather Paffrath would bring me a chocolate bar or a bag of chewy colored candies that stuck to my teeth.

In the spring, Father dug up a larger plot of ground. I liked working with him in the garden. It would be a good summer. But one June morning before dawn, I heard the boots coming up the steps. Father jumped out of bed and threw on his clothes.

"Herr Hamacher, you are under arrest for high treason." The storm trooper grabbed him even before he got the words out of his mouth.

"Why, what have I done?" Father asked. The charge of high treason could mean death.

Even though it was summer, I shivered in my nightgown. I knew he had just returned from an overnight "visit" to friends.

Mother and I stood silent, afraid to speak as we watched them push Father down the steps.

For eight days Mother went from the police station to city hall to the local prisons to find out where the Gestapo had taken him. Everyone was silent. Finally, she found he was in Klingelputz, a much dreaded prison. Mother was called to the Gestapo headquarters for questioning. When she got there, she saw that her father, Grandfather Paffrath, had been called for questioning, too. What would he say? Though he had never forgiven my father for leaving the Catholic church, Grandfather was supportive of Father. He ranted and raged, "Hein is an honest man and a good worker. He's not a criminal."

After a few hours of questioning, both Mother and Grandfather were released.

For three months, no one was allowed to visit Father. Once a week I had to write a letter. It was hard knowing what to write. I loved my father so much, and I had so much to tell him. But it's hard for an eight-year-old to find the proper words.

When we were permitted to visit him, Mother brought him clean clothing. His family gave us money so he could buy food from the guards. One afternoon, she took me with her. Father reached through the bars to clasp my hand. He looked even older than Grandfather. I told him about the cat and Grandfather's jokes.

I hadn't finished before the guard came over and said, "Your ten minutes are up. You'll have to leave."

A few days later, as I was coming home from school, I saw two men from the Gestapo pushing Mother into a car. I froze. I wanted to scream, but the sound stuck in my throat. What would they do to her? Where should I go? A neighbor pulled me into her apartment and sent for my grandmother.

At the prison, a friendly guard told Father, "The Gestapo arrested your wife. She's here, in Klingelputz prison."

"Oh, my God," Father moaned, knowing how the Gestapo tortured people to get them to talk. He knew both he and Mother would be doomed if she told what she knew about his activities with the underground. He kept thinking, she won't be able to hold out. They'll threaten to send Grete away and she'll talk.

But the Gestapo could get nothing from Mother. She kept insisting, "I'm only a housewife. I tend to my sewing and my child. If I knew anything, I'd tell you, just to be with my child." The Gestapo released her.

When Grandfather Paffrath brought Mother back to the apartment, my strong-willed, beautiful blonde-haired mother collapsed on her bed. For weeks, she lay there, unable to move. The tension of the interrogation and her anxiety over what could happen to Father and herself made her collapse. Even though I was a young child, I had to cook and serve her meals in bed. I had to water and weed the garden. Occasionally an aunt or one of my grandmothers would bring us food and help with the housework.

At night, I heard Mother moan in her sleep. "I don't know, I don't know. I have to go home to my child. If I knew, I would tell you."

Even though Father was a "political unreliable" and in prison, I still had to join the *Bund Deutscher Maedel*, the Nazi organization for girls.

I hated going to the meetings. Father had told Mother not to buy me the brown jacket worn by the other girls. "I can't stand the sight of them," he said.

Though I wore the standard white shirt, black tie, and blue skirt, my red sweater marked me as an outsider. I liked the sports and the marching and singing through the villages, and I wanted to be dressed like the others.

In 1937, Father was released. His younger brother, who was a builder, came to see him. "Hein, I can't get any contracts unless I join the Nazi party." My uncle really looked up to my father. He badly wanted his approval. "What does it matter if I join? A piece of paper . . . I'm not really a Nazi, but my family has to eat. Why don't you join, too?"

"If you must, you must," Father said, knowing his brother wanted him to understand what was happening to him.

Though the smokestacks from the chemical plants and Fordworks that surrounded Cologne were going night and day, NOT RECOMMENDED FOR HIRING remained stamped on Father's identity card. Until 1938, he could not get regular work. Every time he was offered a job, he had to show his stamped work papers. After a week he was let go. He

119

worked at a succession of illegal jobs, as a laborer or as a bookkeeper.

My mother, with the help of my grandparents and uncles, started a small business. She sold candies, tea, and coffee. This was a good cover for Father. He delivered packages to customers and secretly exchanged underground information.

By 1938, German preparations for conquering the world were going full blast. Germany had annexed Austria and the Fordworks was turning out trucks. The demand for skilled workers increased. Five years after he had been arrested, Father was permitted to return to his real occupation. The Fordworks was an American firm. They were the only ones hiring "unreliables."

I concentrated on my studies, hoping to go to high school. My parents always said, "Education is power." But the child of a "political unreliable," no matter how good a student, would not be permitted to go to high school. At thirteen, I entered a trade school to study shorthand and typing. In my free time, I went boating with my parents. Sometimes we would tie up to a dock and go swimming at the foot of an ancient castle. We talked and sang and feasted on potato salad and bread. I was careful not to repeat anything I heard.

My mother's family loved to sing. Uncle Willie played the mandolin and Uncle Hans the guitar. On Sundays and holidays, the family would come together just to sing folk songs.

The summer before the war, I was visiting my uncle in Duesseldorf. On August 23, 1939, he suddenly became angry. Hitler had signed a nonaggression treaty with Russia.

"Now we're really going to get into a war," he raged. "Now that he doesn't have to worry about the Russians, he'll attack Poland." I left for home. A week later, Hitler invaded Poland.

As the months passed, I became more and more frightened. Poland, Norway, Denmark, France, Belgium, and Holland all fell to "Our Glorious Reich." With a father who was called a political unreliable, I would never be able to realize my dream of going to a university. There were great celebrations in the streets when Germany turned on its Russian ally on June 22, 1941, and invaded the Ukraine. Newspaper headlines and radio announcers broadcast victory after victory.

Privately, my father was happy when Hitler turned on Russia. "Now the war is lost. Hitler will be fighting on too many fronts," he said.

In 1942 Allied aircraft started to bomb our area. In fascination, my friends and I would rush to the bombed-out sites to see the damage. We'd search for splinters from the bombs so we could trade them as souvenirs.

By 1943, there were attacks almost every night. We slept in our clothing. Our knapsacks, filled with food and water, lay beside our beds. When the alarm sounded we grabbed the knapsacks and rushed down to the basement. We learned to listen for three signals: The first meant aircraft had been sighted coming over the border. The second signaled they were targeting the area around Cologne. The third announced the end of the raid. The nighttime raids always came in the middle of the night. After the third signal, we'd leave. When we came out, the sky was dark from the smoke of all the fires. In one raid, the entire town of Mulheim was leveled. The streets were littered with corpses. Three of my parents' best friends were killed.

In June 1943, I graduated from trade school. It was a difficult time to be a teenager. Though there were a few young men in the factories and some soldiers stationed in the area, it was not the time to hold dances and go out on dates. We could no longer go boating on the Rhine; it was too dangerous. I was hired as a buyer of supplies for the Fordworks. My hours were from seven A.M. to six P.M. five days a week and from seven A.M. to two P.M. on Saturday. I tried to use the long hours as an excuse for not attending meetings of the German Girls' Movement.

One evening, I came home and found a warning. "You are to report to the head of the Bund to explain your absence."

I reported to the Central Office of the Bund. "I'm sorry, but by the time I finish work and help in the garden, I'm exhausted."

"That's no excuse. You must give every ounce of your energy to serve our Fuehrer. If you miss any more meetings, there will be serious consequences."

"Serious consequences" meant prison or a concentration camp, not only for me, but for Father.

The Allies had begun daylight bombings. The nearby chemical plant of Bayer Leverkusen was hit. My father felt elated. "If the Allied bombers can get through to strike Cologne, then the Nazis must be losing."

On July 21, 1944, at 5:30 A.M., the boots of the Gestapo sounded on the stairs. Father had already left for the factory. The day before, July 20, a bomb had been exploded in an attempt to kill Hitler. Unfortunately, just before the bomb went off, someone had moved the briefcase containing the bomb. Hitler survived. A witch hunt began. Several generals who had instigated the bombing were rounded up. The Gestapo arrested anyone with a record of "political unreliability." When the Gestapo found that Father was not home, they raced toward the factory.

I hopped on my bicycle and pedaled the nine miles to the plant. I had to warn Father. Just as I reached the main gate, I saw two members of the Gestapo escorting Father to their car. The car turned toward Cologne.

I went to the political office in the factory. "Where are they taking my father? He's done nothing wrong."

The political officer refused to give me an answer. He accused me of disloyalty because I had been absent from meetings of the League of German Girls.

When I returned home, I found Mother frantic. She had gone to the various authorities, but no one would tell her where Father was. Later, she found he had been rounded up with several hundred people and held in the Cologne exhibition hall. In September, bruised and beaten, he was released for lack of evidence. Our joy was short lived. Orders came for Father to report to the Volksturm, the peoples' army. Despite a 50 percent disability for wounds suffered in World War I, he would have to fight. Millions of German soldiers had been killed on the Russian front, but Hitler refused to surrender. He wanted every German to die fighting for the Fatherland. Old men and thirteen- and fourteen-year-olds were to defend the cities. Father had to disappear.

By 1945, Allied bombers had turned Cologne into huge mounds of bricks and jagged glass. Crowds of people were frantically clawing through the ruins of their demolished apartments in search of their loved ones.

The distant sound of cannons told us that the Americans were approaching. Members of the Resistance spotted the German army planting explosives under the railroad bridges of Cologne. For several nights, Father and one of his brothers stole out of Father's hiding place to remove them before they could be set off. My two uncles, who had joined the Nazi party, tossed their party cards into the fireplace. German soldiers took off their uniforms and tried to disappear.

The day American trucks entered Cologne, we hung white sheets in the window to welcome the American soldiers. Everyone stood outside the house and cheered.

Even before the armistice was signed, Father and his friends met to reorganize the Social Democratic party. Once again, I heard Father's footsteps bouncing down the steps as he rushed from our apartment to his party meetings. My mother continued to be his partner. She believed what her Hein believed, helping and encouraging him, managing the household on very little money. Without her help, he would not have been able to accomplish what he did.

In 1947, he was elected a representative to the Cologne city council. Ten years later, he was elected to represent the Cologne South District in the Bundestag, the West German congress.

After the war, Grete Hamacher von Loesch completed her

high school education and obtained a degree in economics from the University of Marburg. From 1968 to 1989 she was a member of the Frankfurt city council. Her husband, Dr. Achim von Loesch, is the director of a bank. The Von Loesches have a daughter who is a doctor and a son who is a musician.

PART V
Slaves for the Nazi Empire

10

Ondřej: A Czech Schoolboy Fights Back

> OPERATION GREEN (Plan to invade
> Czechoslovakia): When Germany has achieved
> complete preparedness for war . . . military
> conditions will have been created for carrying
> out an offensive war against Czechoslovakia, so
> the solution of the German problem of living
> space can be carried to a victorious conclusion.
> — General Jodl, Army Chief of Operation
> Staff, December 7, 1937

In *Mein Kampf*, Hitler told of his master plan to create a vast German empire in central Europe, reaching from the English Channel and the Baltic Sea far into Russia. This empire would swallow the small countries in its path, such as Poland, Austria, Czechoslovakia, Rumania, and Hungary. The master plan seemed too unrealistic to be believed.

But step by step, Hitler set out to achieve his goals. His first action was to test whether the western powers, England and France, had the guts to oppose him. The Versailles Treaty of World War I limited Germany to an army of a hundred thousand men. It also limited the number and size of German warships. In 1934, Hitler ordered the German army tripled in number and the construction of additional and larger warships.

The western powers did nothing.

The Versailles Treaty had also called for the demilitarization of the west bank of the Rhine River. This part of Germany, facing France, was to be a buffer zone with no military facilities. In 1936, Hitler's troops marched into the Rhineland.

The western powers did nothing.

In March 1938, Hitler overthrew the government of Austria and made that country part of the Greater Reich (greater Germany). Austria ceased to exist.

The western powers did nothing.

Now Hitler turned to Czechoslovakia, a newly formed republic that had been created by the Allies after World War I. It was taken from a part of the Austro-Hungarian empire. In addition to two principal nationalities, the Czechs from Bohemia and Moravia and the Slovaks, who occupied Slovakia, there were pockets of Hungarians, Ruthenians, and Sudeten Germans. Czechoslovakia, which was blessed with good leaders, was one of the most prosperous and democratic countries in Europe.

The three and a half million Sudeten Germans had never been part of Germany, but they spoke German. They felt a kinship to Germany. Hitler accused the Czech government of mistreating the Sudeten Germans and he threatened to attack Czechoslovakia unless the area called Sudetenland were ceded to Germany.

Czechoslovakia had a good army and strong defensive positions on its German border. The Czechs also had a defensive alliance with France and Russia. However, the Russians could not intervene without crossing Polish territory, and Poland refused to let the Russians enter. Czechoslovakia had to depend on France and her ally, Great Britain, to defend it.

The combined armies of Czechoslovakia, France, and England were three times the size of the German army. German generals feared that an attack on Czechoslovakia would mean the defeat of Germany. Some generals even offered secret advice to England to stand firm against Hitler. If England did, Hitler would have to back down.

In spite of the generals' advice, the Prime Minister of Great Britain, Neville Chamberlain, and the Prime Minister of France, Edouard Daladier, went to Germany to negotiate with Hitler. They were desperate for peace. World War I had ended only twenty years before, and both countries had lost millions of men.

Hitler, a shrewd politician, sensed this weakness. His demands went up and up. In the end, Chamberlain and Daladier agreed to give him the Sudetenland. On October 1, 1938, German troops occupied the territory.

The strong Czech defensive positions, which were in the Sudetenland, were now in German hands. Czechoslovakia was without military defenses, and its supposed protectors had turned their backs. In March 1939, Hitler seized the rest of Czechoslovakia. The independent nation ceased to exist.

By this time, it was too late to stop Hitler. Each time he had challenged the western powers, he had triumphed. On September 1, 1939, he attacked Poland. World War II had begun. The nations that had sought to avoid a war by giving away Czechoslovakia now found themselves on the firing line.

Ondřej Laska, the son of a Czech diplomat, was one who fought back.

"You can't arrest my sons. They're American citizens." Father stood in the living room, in his nightshirt, arguing with two S.S. men. I had been asleep when they began to pound on the door.

"Just a routine check," the taller S.S. man, who had a scar across his right cheek, assured Father. "The whole family will accompany us to the station." The shorter S.S. man put his hand on his holster. The two Czech policemen with them looked embarrassed.

My twin brother, Vaclav, and I stood there in our pajamas, still dazed from the five A.M. awakening. Mother switched on another lamp.

The double lightning insignia on the taller man's collar shone in the light. "Get dressed quickly."

How would being Americans keep two eleven-year-olds from being arrested? Vaclav and I had been born in Cleveland, Ohio, when my father was Czechoslovakian consul to the United States, but we were Czech like our parents. Being part American was a pain in the neck. We were five years old when Father was reassigned to Prague. The first day of kindergarten, the other kids made fun of our half-Czech–half-American vocabulary. "Greaseballs, where did you learn Czech? Go back to where you came from."

I came home from school with a black eye. "It's nothing," I insisted. "The guy who hit me has two black eyes."

Mother put a cold compress on my eye.

"Did you start the fight, Andy?" my father asked. He had just returned from the Foreign Office to get ready for a party. He put his briefcase on the dining room table and examined my eye.

"No, he called me names." My eye really stung but I wouldn't cry.

Father put his arm around me. "Andy, I'm proud of you. I don't want you ever to start a fight, but I expect you to always defend yourself."

Vaclav and I had no trouble defending ourselves. We were both stocky and loved sports. As soon as we could walk, Father put us on a horse. He took us swimming in the Vltava River and taught us all kinds of water sports.

Father hung his coat in the closet and put his hat on the shelf. "We'll start the boxing lessons tonight."

The bullies soon learned we could defend ourselves.

A short while later, Father was assigned to Algiers, North Africa. The first day of school, an Arab student lunged at me with a knife. "Foreigners, infidels, get out of Algeria."

I put up my fists and felt blood on my arm. Vaclav tripped the boy, and we ran home.

"What's an infidel?" I shouted, as I stumbled into the apartment, my shirt torn and bloody.

Mother had just returned from a tea. She was wearing a pale yellow dress. "Quick, some hot water and soap," she called to the maid in the kitchen. As she cleansed the wound, bright red spots stained her dress. "An infidel is someone who does not believe in the same religion that you do."

That night, our parents came home from their party early. Father pushed aside the living room furniture. He took three dinner knives from a box. "Now I'll teach you how to disarm an opponent with a knife."

We practiced that whole evening. Father had been a hero

133

in the Czech Resistance against Germany during World War I. He knew self-defense, and his adventures had been written up in books. I loved to read about them.

Despite the taunts of our classmates, we liked having a father in the diplomatic service. Many times, when he had to travel throughout Africa, he took us with him. I loved the long auto rides across the desert to visit the Roman ruins. Father was wild about hunting. Often we rode on camels to shoot deer in the Atlas Mountains. Vaclav and I agreed that no one could have a more exciting job than Father.

Until September 29, 1938. Late in the afternoon, Father rushed into the apartment white-faced. "France and England have just handed the Sudetenland to Hitler," he said.

Mother stared at Father in disbelief. "How could they?"

"Those imbeciles!" He slammed his fist on the desk. He raged as he told us the British and the French had given away Czechoslovakia's coal, iron, and steel industries. Czech munitions plants were now in German hands.

Mother's usually smiling face turned serious. "You're known as an anti-Nazi. You'll be among the first to be arrested if they seize the rest of the country. We'd better leave for America at once."

Father stared at the suit of armor standing opposite his desk. It had been worn by a Crusader. "Yes. It's only a matter of time before they do."

His letter of resignation, via diplomatic pouch, went off to Prague that evening.

A month later, the head of the Foreign Office asked him to remain in North Africa "long enough to liquidate the affairs of the Czechoslovakian office of Consul General."

Mother protested. "No, it's too dangerous. We can't risk endangering the boys." She had read *Mein Kampf*. Hitler had promised to destroy Czechoslovakia.

"Maria, I have always served the Czech government. A few more months won't matter."

Mother began to organize the packing. Vaclav and I stuck the Roman coins we had picked up on the beach into our suitcases.

In February 1939, we returned to Prague to wrap up Father's affairs. Since we expected to stay only three months, we rented a furnished apartment. We had visas for America and tickets for the end of April on a British liner, the *Queen Mary*. Would Vaclav and I be "foreigners" again?

On March 15, even before we could dress for breakfast, we heard the rumble of tanks. We threw on our overcoats and ran outside. Panzer tanks, followed by other armored vehicles, rolled through the cobblestone streets of Prague. Behind them goose-stepped column after column of helmeted infantrymen. Women stood in the light rain, sobbing. Father's face was grim.

Now, only three days after the invasion, the Gestapo stood in our living room. Vaclav and I had already laid out our clothes for school the night before. We dressed quickly.

Father tried to reassure us. "It's obvious with the Czech policemen accompanying them, they'll take us to the Czech police station. A few questions, and they'll let us go."

It was still dark when we climbed into the police van. Mother held on to our hands as though we were little boys. The van stopped in front of the Gestapo headquarters.

"They lied," my father said under his breath.

The scar-faced S.S. man grabbed Father by the arm.

"Herr Laska, you are to come with me. Your family will be fine as long as you cooperate."

"Maria, take care of the boys," Father called as he disappeared into a room.

My mother's fingers clamped so tightly around my arm they hurt.

The shorter S.S. man tried to release Mother's fingers. "The boys are to follow me."

"No. Call the American consul. They're Americans. I demand you release us at once."

He again tried to loosen her fingers. "You are making it difficult for yourself."

Mother's eyes were like those of a tigress. "Shame on you. They're eleven years old. They've committed no crime."

The S.S. man shoved Mother to the floor. Before we could help her, two policemen grabbed us and pushed us into the van.

We heard Mother's screams as we were driven away from the Gestapo headquarters. This was the first time we had ever been forcibly separated from our parents.

"Andy, what do you think they'll do to Father? What will happen to Mother?"

"I don't know." Where were they taking us? Would we ever see our parents again?

The van stopped in front of a gray fortress, a juvenile detention center. "Here's where we put scum like you," the driver said. The sun was just starting to rise. Would we ever again get up before dawn and go hunting with Father?

"Laska, Vaclav and Ondřej, six months." The sergeant in charge was munching on a white roll. I remembered we hadn't eaten breakfast. The key clanked as the door to the cell block opened. Inside, there were rows of cells, each filled with bunk beds and a bucket. Most of the boys were still asleep. They looked older than we were.

One of them gave a low whistle. "What do you know, gentlemen in fancy overcoats! And the shine on your shoes could light up St. Stephens. Think you were going to a party?" His shirt was torn and I couldn't figure out the color. "Welcome, gentlemen, I'm Peter. And why were you invited to join us for tea?"

Father had taught us to be polite to everyone, even when they weren't polite to us. "Our father is with the Foreign Service."

Vaclav interrupted. "And he fought against the Germans in the war. He's famous. Our whole family was arrested this morning. We don't know why we're here."

Peter turned over on his cot. "Slave labor, that's why." He went back to sleep.

I didn't believe him. Slaves were in Roman times. At seven o'clock, a bell rang.

"On your feet, you lazy bums," the guard said. He marched us to the railroad yard. "You're to unload these cartons from the boxcars and carry them on your backs to the warehouse four blocks away."

The heaviest thing I had ever carried was Father's hunting rifle. The boxes seemed to weigh fifty pounds. By the end of the day, Vaclav and I could hardly move one foot in front of the other.

"If you're too tired to eat," Peter said, when the guard brought us a bowl of stew, "I'll eat it for you."

The stew smelled terrible, not like Mother's with big

137

pieces of meat and potatoes. "Vaclav, we've got to make a pact," I said. "We have to promise to eat everything they give us to stay alive. We have to be brave like Father."

Our chief task, when we weren't carrying heavy loads, was to sweep the streets with straw brooms. Our white shirts soon turned as gray as the cobblestones.

The six months of our sentence seemed to drag on and on. One day, I asked the guard, "When will you let us go?"

"Shut up. You'll get out when we're good and ready, or else in a coffin."

I was frightened and angry. "Vaclav, always try to act like Father."

One morning, before dawn, we were awakened by the turn of the key. "Boys, wipe your noses," the guard said. "You're going home to your momma."

Mother, who had been imprisoned for only a few days, had finally arranged through friends for our release. It was a joyous but subdued reunion.

Our first thoughts were of Father. "Where is he? Is he all right?"

She shook her head. "No one will tell me anything. I've been to all the authorities, but they won't give me any news."

It was late 1939, and the war had broken out in Poland in September. We took the streetcar to school, as though nothing had been disturbed in our lives. We missed Father terribly. I began, almost by instinct, to drop by the apartment of Professor Ogoun, whose son Luba was in my class. After I had been there a few times, Professor Ogoun said, "Andy, you are the son of a patriot. You know how to keep your mouth shut. Let me show you something."

He took me behind a false wall he had built in front of the windows of his apartment. During the war, everyone had to black out the windows to keep light from shining through. Since his windows jutted out of the apartment, he blacked them out and then built a long room in front of the windows. Then he covered the wall with black-out material, as though it were a window. When members of the resistance needed a place to stay, he hid them behind the false windows.

Over the years, I got used to seeing strangers in his apartment. He never introduced them by name, but I soon realized they were members of the Resistance. My friend Jan Haida was the son of a butcher. Jan and I carried meat in our schoolbags to help feed the guests. Occasionally, I would pedal my bike to a farm and steal fruit from the trees to feed them.

Toward the end of May 1942, Jan and I dropped by the Ogouns'. Two visitors whom I had never seen before emerged from the secret room. From their conversation, I learned they had come from London. I knew enough not to ask how or why. But I figured out they must be on some mission for the Resistsance.

"We've got to get them raincoats," Professor Ogoun said. "In this wet weather, they'll look suspicious going about without them."

One of the men was my height. "He can use mine," I said. "I have Father's."

"Here's my cap," Jan said, putting it on the table. "Come on, let's go get your coat."

As the trolley we were riding rounded the corner, we saw seven men and three women being led to a gallows the Nazis had set up in front of the church.

"More reprisals!" I said, so angry I wanted to jump off and fight the Germans with my bare hands.

Jan touched my shoulder. "No matter how many hostages they take, we'll still fight back."

The Resistance had stepped up its activities since Reinhard Heydrich, the "Blond Beast" and head of the Gestapo, had been named Protector of Bohemia and Moravia. In a secret meeting Heydrich promised to "eliminate" the Czechs. Germany wanted our land for Germans.

On May 27, 1942, when I turned on the radio, I heard, "A bomb was thrown into the car of Obergruppenfuhrer Reinhard Heydrich. Fortunately, he was only wounded. Authorities are searching for the two traitors who attempted to murder him. Appropriate measures will be taken to apprehend all who assisted them."

The newspapers carried descriptions of the "assassins." A photograph showed three items that had been found at the scene of the crime. A raincoat, a cap, and a bicycle. The raincoat was mine. The cap belonged to Jan. "These items will be displayed in the department store window at Wenceslaus Square. Anyone who can identify the owners will receive a reward of ten million crowns."

After school, Jan and I took a streetcar to Wenceslaus Square. As we stared at the coat and cap, he nudged me. "The underground removed the labels."

Heydrich died two days later. In reprisal, the Germans razed the village of Lidice and killed all the men. The women were deported to concentration camps. The children were either killed or sent to Germany for re-education. Massive arrests and executions followed. When the Gestapo came to Professor Ogoun's apartment, they found nothing.

Despite the reprisals, the resolve of the Resistance grew. After school I delivered messages and scouted the countryside on my bike for food. My activities ended abruptly when two soldiers came into the classroom.

They began to read off a list of names of "political unreliables." "Laska, Ondřej; Laska, Vaclav . . ."

With the other "unreliables," we were sent to the coal mines in Kladno, in western Czechoslovakia. The mine extended a mile into the earth. In the freezing cold, we carried our picks and axes down into the dark tunnels. Our only light came from small lamps. I worried about Vaclav. He had had rheumatic fever as a child. How long could he stand the cold and work? Many of our classmates had dropped from exhaustion. The Germans shot those who could no longer work.

Our mining careers ended six months later, when we were shipped to the Polish border. For the first time in the war, the Germans were being driven back. In order to stop the Russian advance, the labor force was taken to a flat area to dig antitank ditches. There were no "hours." We shoveled earth until we had dug the allotted number of ditches for that day.

One afternoon, the man in front of me fainted and fell face down into a puddle. I knew he would die if I didn't lift him out of the water. I dropped to my knees to help him. The guard hit me over the head with his rifle. I collapsed on top of the man. As I lay there, blood trickled down my neck. I felt my skull. It was cracked. I had to get up. To stay meant death. Vaclav was working with another group. There was no way of calling him. I had terrible pains in my eye. I staggered to my feet, the pain increasing with each movement. I kept thinking of my father. He would have forced himself to go on. Finally I caught up with the group.

That night as I lay on the straw mattress in the bunk, I knew I had to escape. If I didn't I would surely die. After a few days, when the pain was not quite so sharp, I saw an opportunity to get away. In the otherwise flat land, there was a slight mound of earth a few feet away from where I worked. It was dark, and the Germans had turned on searchlights so we could work. Every time the light shifted to another area, I started digging a shallow grave in the side of the mound. When the guard shouted "Return to camp," I lay down in the grave and covered myself with dirt.

The column disappeared. I jumped out of the grave and ran to the nearest town. I climbed on a freight train going toward Poland. When the Germans found I was missing, I was sure they would search the trains heading for Czechoslovakia.

"If ever you're in trouble," Professor Ogoun had said, "go to a railroad yard. In every country, the workers are with the Resistance."

Twenty miles later, when the train slowed down to round a curve, I jumped off. The local railroad workers fed me and hid me under some coal on a train going toward Czechoslovakia. When we crossed the border, I tumbled off the train.

Czech railroad workers found me and carried me to the cabin of the leader of the local Resistance group. Delirious, I fell into his arms babbling, "My brother, my brother, I have to rescue my brother." Then I fell unconscious.

When I woke up, my head was bandaged. When I recovered, I found the worst part about being in the Resistance was sitting around the cabin waiting for orders. Day after day, I played chess or bridge with the others who were hiding out with me.

One night, I went back to help Vaclav escape. It was days before I reached the site of the camp. I found the barracks abandoned.

I knocked at a nearby farmhouse. "What happened to the prisoners?"

"The front was coming too close. All the boys were sent back home — those who were still alive."

I had to see if Vaclav was safe. I walked for several days, sleeping in barns and bombed-out buildings to get to Prague. Late one night, I sneaked into my mother's apartment.

"Thank God," Vaclav said when he answered the door and hugged me. "Somehow I knew you were still alive." He was dressed in a tie and jacket, very much the schoolboy.

Mother rushed over and took me in her arms. "Father's still in prison, but we're all alive, thank God." She didn't know what to do first, feed me or fetch water for me to wash. My clothes, stiffened by mud and rain, smelled like the coal cars I had slept in.

I knew I could stay only a short while, but I didn't know how to tell Mother. A few days later, I looked up from my bed. She was packing my rucksack. "There's enough bread and meat to last you a week. I know you must rejoin your Resistance group. Your father will be proud of you."

How I admired Mother. I knew how difficult it was for her to let me leave.

By December 1944, Russian troops had reached eastern Czechoslovakia. In the village below our hideout, the Germans operated a munitions plant. If the Russians got too close, they were planning to blow it up. The explosion would have destroyed the whole village. Several of us got jobs in the plant. For months we searched for the explosives and successfully defused them.

When we heard that the liberation was starting in Prague, we hijacked an armored train. A German plane spotted us and began to pepper us with bullets. We dashed under the train until the attack stopped.

On May 5, 1945, my Resistance unit reached northern Prague. The Czech Resistance had decided to try to seize Prague from the Germans. They ordered all Resistance units into battle.

I climbed to the top of a roof to pick off German soldiers. My commander signaled for me to come down. "Look, kid, you speak English. There are two American tanks just outside the city. Eisenhower sent them from Pilsen to find out what's happening. Tell them to get the hell over here and help us."

I made my way to the American tanks.

"Sorry, kid," the sergeant said when he received the message. "We have orders to let the Russians take the city. Some kind of agreement at Yalta."

The Russians were throwing all their men and firepower

into the battle of Berlin. It would be days before they could launch an assault on Prague. Thousands of Czechs lay dead. We were running out of ammunition. In the five days of fighting, only a Russian renegade, General Vlasov, helped us. Vlasov had been an officer in the Russian army, but he hated Joseph Stalin, the Russian leader. When Vlasov was captured at the battle of Stalingrad, he offered to form an army unit to fight with the Germans against the Russians. The unit was made up of anti-Communist Russian prisoners of war from Lithuania and the Ukraine. Now Vlasov had decided to switch sides again and used the German tanks and ammunition against the Germans.

On May 9, 1945, the Russian forces entered Prague. The battle was over. But the war did not end for me. An explosive bullet from a German who had not yet surrendered tore up my right thigh. I woke up in a hospital. I stared, overjoyed, at Father. "You're alive!"

He bent down and kissed my forehead.

Ondřej Laska was awarded a Medal of Valor for his activities in the Resistance. After the war, he became an American citizen. He has had a distinguished career as an international businessman. He is married to Dr. Vera Laska, a historian who also fought with the Czech Resistance.

11

Zbigniew: The Underground Medical School in Poland

Kill without pity or mercy all men, women,
and children of Polish descent or language.
Only in this way can we obtain the living
space we need.
— Adolf Hitler

For centuries Germany coveted the fertile fields of Poland.
In *Mein Kampf*, Hitler openly stated his intention to occupy
all Eastern European nations in order to provide *lebensraum*
(living room) for the German empire he planned to create.
To justify his invasion of Poland, Hitler declared all Slavic
peoples — Poles, Lithuanians, Ukrainians, Latvians,
Czechs, Estonians, and Russians — *untermenschen* (subhuman).

The regular German army, in its invasion of Poland, had
orders to kill as many civilians as possible. In addition,
there was a second German army whose job was not to
take territory but to kill. These killing squads, the *Einsatzgruppen*, were made up of members of the security section
of the S.S. and the Gestapo. The *Einsatzgruppen* followed
directly behind the regular troops. Once a town was taken,
the *Einsatzgruppen* rounded up Jews, Gypsies, and any
Poles who had at least a high school education. Those
seized were either shot or put in mobile vans and gassed.

Jews and Gypsies not killed immediately were forced into ghettos to await their final destruction.

In their determination to destroy any potential leaders, the Germans rounded up officials, teachers, lawyers, doctors, merchants, and priests. In the city of Bydgoszcz, Boy Scouts ages twelve to sixteen were shot.

The only Poles exempt from the death threat were blue-eyed, blond-haired children. Over two hundred thousand children were torn from their parents and sent to special homes in Germany. They were given new names and raised as Nazis. The dark-haired Polish children were to be taught only "simple arithmetic, writing one's own name; the lesson that it is a divine commandment to be obedient to the Germans . . . I do not think reading is required," said Heinrich Himmler, head of the S.S.

While elementary schools were permitted, the Germans closed Poland's high schools and universities. Anyone caught teaching high school or college subjects was executed. Poland, a country that had been invaded many times, had had a long history of resistance to foreign authorities. When it was forbidden to teach the Polish language or Polish history and customs, Polish teachers organized secret classes. During the Nazi invasion, Polish youth attended classes in attics, basements, barns, churches, and private homes. In addition to high schools, three secret medial schools were established.

The largest was disguised as a school for sanitary personnel. Dr. Jan Zaorski, a prominent doctor and professor, convinced the German authorities to allow him to set up a school to train sanitary workers. The Germans, who feared epidemics and water pollution, agreed. With former professors from the University of Warsaw, Dr. Zaorski conducted classes in anatomy, physiology, and other medical subjects. Laboratories were set up, and corpses found on the streets were used for dissection in basements. Between 1940 and the Polish Uprising in 1944, over nineteen hundred students secretly studied medicine. Unfortunately, only a small percentage of these students survived the war.

In 1940, fifty professors from the University of Poznan, who had fled to Warsaw, established the University of the Western Territories. The carefully screened students took an oath of secrecy before being admitted to the school. All students and professors had to take assumed names. The location of the classes, which were held in private homes, changed each week.

The third school existed in the Warsaw Ghetto. The Germans had imprisoned Warsaw's half million Jews in a walled section of the city. In 1940, Professor J. Zweibaum, a Jewish doctor, got permission to train students and physicians in the control of epidemics. Because the inhabitants of the ghetto were being starved to death on 300 calories a day, the streets were littered with corpses. The situation was ripe for a typhus epidemic. To prevent plagues, the Germans allowed Dr. Zweibaum to instruct workers in basic sanitary techniques. With other Jewish doctors, including the world-famous hematologist-serologist, Dr. Ludwig Hirszfeld, he secretly provided the "sanitary workers" with a medical education. At the completion of each course, examinations were given. The instructors hoped that, through some miracle, some of the students would survive and practice medicine. The school was disbanded in 1942 when the Germans began the final evacuation of the Warsaw Ghetto. Most of the students and teachers were deported to the death camps. Out of five hundred students, only fifty survived.

Despite the terrible conditions, several of the doctors in the ghetto recorded the gradual effects of starvation on a population. A monograph was smuggled out of the ghetto and after the war, the studies were published in a book, *The Disease of Hunger*, now a medical classic.

It is a monument to the spirit and stubbornness of the Polish people that all three secret medical schools existed in a heavily occupied city. The schools lacked proper textbooks, medical supplies, and medicines. The clinical training had to be taken in hospitals where the students were disguised as nurses, janitors, and stretcher bearers. If discovered, students and teachers would have been put to death.

Zbigniew Zawadzki was one of the few among the nineteen hundred students of the University of Warsaw Medical School who lived to recount the story of his education under fire.

———•———

Just before dawn, the sirens jolted me out of bed. Across the street, the Church of the Redemption burst into flames. The ground shook as German dive bombers scored one direct hit after another on schools and government buildings.

"It's war," I shouted, as I grabbed my clothes. "Come on, let's drop off our applications. As soon as we lick the Germans, school will start." I dashed down the steps. My two friends followed.

Our landlady stood in the doorway screaming and shaking her fists. "My son, my son. He's in the army. What's to become of him?"

Still buttoning my shirt, I ran toward the University of Warsaw. A woman carrying a child in each arm pleaded with two other children to hold tightly to her skirt as she struggled through the frantic crowd toward the air raid shelter. It was September 1, 1939, and the accumulated heat of summer hung over the motionless air.

What was I doing, submitting my application to medical school? Stubbornly, I pushed toward the university. My dream of becoming a doctor began when I was fifteen. I had had a perforated appendix and the doctors told my mother to call a priest. Despite the fact they felt there was no hope, the doctors drained my abdomen and saved me.

I was determined to register for medical school, and a war was not going to stop me. I was convinced that the Polish army would quickly defeat the Germans and my life would return to normal. I was eighteen, and in a hurry to become a doctor.

We dropped off our applications and pushed our way through the crowds to the recruiting office on Aleje Jerozolimskie. It was hard to squeeze into the store-front room. Every young man in Warsaw was trying to enlist. The sergeant threw up his hands. "I can't sign you up. The army's on the run. I'll let you know when I get my orders." The sergeant's collar dripped with sweat as he wrote down our names and addresses.

For two days, the world watched as the Polish cavalry

fought German tanks. Finally, on September 3, France and England declared war on Germany. The war would soon be over, and medical school would start in a few weeks.

My optimism was shattered when I turned on the radio. "All men of fighting age are to leave the city and head east. Warsaw will be defended to the last bastion. Long live Poland!" It didn't make sense. Why were we ordered to leave if we were supposed to defend the city?

As we started to throw our stuff in our rucksacks, a friend bounded up the steps. "Don't go. The government is forming an underground army to infiltrate behind the enemy lines. If we're caught —" he drew his finger across his neck. "On the other hand, a bomb can kill you, too."

I joined the "*Dyversants* (the underground army)." Instead of studying anatomy, I learned how to garrote a German soldier and to make explosives powerful enough to blow up bridges and barracks. My first assignment was to guard the abandoned headquarters of the General Inspectorate of the Polish Army (GISZ). The basement was loaded with ammunition. Whenever the air-raid sirens sounded, everyone ran across Aleja Szucha, one of the most beautiful streets in Warsaw, and flung himself on the grass. Between the raids, my unit drilled while we waited to be slipped behind enemy lines.

One morning, there was a scary quiet. No planes. No bombs. Just the "chirp, chirp" of crickets.

Minutes later, we saw a car drive down the maple-lined street. It was our Polish commander. "Attention!" He looked defeated. "An armistice has been signed. The war is over. You are free to go wherever you want."

The Germans took control of the radio stations. "All

Poles are to lay down their arms. All radios are to be turned over to German authorities. Anyone caught with a gun or radio will be shot."

My friends and I decided to return home to Sosnowiec. We stuffed our knapsacks with army biscuits and filled our canteens with water. At the railroad yard, we jumped on a cattle car heading west. Hundreds of young men crowded the seats and aisles trying to escape from Warsaw. Before we could reach Sosnowiec, a German roadblock forced the train to stop.

"Everyone out," a German officer shouted. His whip lashed out at us, as though we were cattle. "Line up, in groups of five. Forward march."

Where were they taking us? To be shot or to Germany? I stared at the soldier walking beside our group. He didn't look like the stereotyped picture of a blond, blue-eyed Nazi. He was stoop shouldered and wore glasses. We stared at one another.

As the column started to turn the corner, he whispered, "*Raus* (out)."

"Let's go," I said to my friends. We ducked behind the hedge and into a small garden. When the guards and prisoners passed by, we jumped across the garden hedges separating the backyards that led to the railroad station. We hopped on a freight train. Several hours later, I reached Sosnowiec.

"Thank God you're alive," my mother said. She hugged me as though she would never let go. "First I feed you *pierozki*, and then we talk."

My aunt brought a platter of the hot dumplings. "I heard

that the Jagiellonian University will open in Krakow in a few days. Why not enroll there?"

My friends and I immediately made plans to attend the opening-day ceremonies. But the day before we were to leave, I caught the flu. I was heartbroken when they left without me, but my illness was a blessing for me.

The Germans surrounded the school and deported all of the students and faculty to the Sachsenhausen concentration camp. Most of them did not survive.

I joined the Sosnowiec detachment of the Armia Krajowa, the underground army. For almost a year, I took part in actions, derailing trains carrying supplies for German soldiers and raiding German arsenals. One night, a member of our group was caught stealing ration cards. The Germans went from house to house looking for other members of the Resistance. The soil of Sosnowiec became "too hot." I had to get out of Poland.

By this time, it was September 1940. The hopes of a quick Allied victory had vanished. My goal was to join Polish army units that were now attached to the British army. With two friends, I leaped aboard a freight train. We jumped off at the base of the Carpathian Mountains. My mother had given me some money and I negotiated with two guides to take us over the mountains into Hungary. From neutral Hungary we hoped somehow to reach the Allied forces.

The guides left us in a wooded area. As we walked down a path, I saw a man sitting under a tree and eating lunch.

"Where are we?" I naïvely asked. "And which way to the Yugoslavian border?"

The man brushed the crumbs from his jacket. "Follow me." He led us directly to the police station.

The police immediately determined that we were Polish and a guard led us toward the railroad station. "Wait here," the guard said as he took each of my friends by the arm. "I'll be back once I put them on the train." As soon as he stepped on the train, I ducked under the platform and into the woods.

I ran south toward the Hungarian town of Koszyce. The guard tracked me down and personally escorted me to the Polish border. "Good riddance," he said as he handed me over to the Germans.

The Germans put me in a cattle car filled with Ukrainians. The Ukrainians wanted to escape from Russia and fight with the German army. As the train headed east, snow began to fall. I shivered in my wet jacket and I nudged Mikhail, the Ukrainian teenager sitting next to me. "When the train slows down, jump."

We bolted over the side and ran into the mountains. After a few days of searching for nuts and berries in the snow, I realized we had to risk going into town, even if it was occupied by the Germans. I tore up my Polish identity papers. "Here, trade me your embroidered shirt for my knapsack. I'll say I'm a Ukrainian who lost his papers."

No sooner had we entered the town, than German soldiers arrested us and took us to the local Gestapo.

"Ukrainians?" The Gestapo chief spat. "I don't have time to fool with two lousy prisoners. Take them back to the town next to the border. The Gestapo is making up a shipment of Ukrainians. They'll take care of them."

By then I knew it was better to take my chances in the

mountains than to trust the Germans. The snow had turned into a heavy rain. "If we get a chance, run for it," I told Mikhail.

"That's crazy," Mikhail responded. "The guard will shoot us."

As the guard, a man in his fifties, led us toward the next town, I stared at him. "You don't look like a Nazi. You look more like a man from here, a decent man. Let us go."

He shook his fist. "Those murderers. They shipped my son off to Germany. Wait until we come to the woods."

As we approached a stand of trees, he raised his thumb over his shoulder. We dashed into the forest. The guard shouted and soon I heard the barking of dogs. However, I knew the dogs would lose our scent in the rain.

We decided to separate. Mikhail fled north. I followed the streams leading toward a village outside of Lublin, Poland. The townspeople took me in. With no paved roads, the town of Chruslanki Josefowskie was an ideal place to hide. To prevent the Germans from seizing their men for forced labor or reprisals, the townspeople set up a lookout. Only Germans had cars. If a car tried to drive down the dirt path, the lookout got on his bike and rode from farmhouse to farmhouse warning the men to hide.

For a year, I worked in the village as a farmhand. In the early summer of 1941, we noticed hundreds of German tanks and thousands of soldiers moving toward the Russian border. The soldiers looked arrogant and very sure of themselves. On June 22, 1941, the Germans invaded Russia, their former ally.

A few weeks later, I received a message through the underground from a former high school classmate. "Warsaw

University has established a secret medical school. Join me, and I'll share everything I have with you."

Study to become a doctor? The Germans said that Poles weren't to be educated. We were to be slaves for our German masters.

"Zbigniew," the farmer said as he put his arm around me, "you are blessed with an education. Poland needs every doctor it can get." He started to fill burlap bags with potatoes, wheat, rye, and buckwheat. "This will help you to stay alive." His horse-drawn cart took us to the Vistula River where I boarded a boat for Warsaw. As I stood on the stern and watched the wake, I wondered. How was it possible for an underground medical school to exist?

The school existed by subterfuge. The "medical" school was not a medical school in the eyes of the Germans. It was the Docent Jan Zaorski's School for Sanitary Personnel.

Dr. Zaorski had convinced the Germans to set up a sanitary department to prevent epidemics and to insure a clean supply of water. Since able-bodied Germans were fighting on the Russian front, a Polish professor was permitted to head the department. Dr. Zaorski insisted that "sanitary" workers had to have courses in chemistry, anatomy, physiology, and other medical subjects.

While it was exciting to be in medical school, Warsaw was a total jungle. At any time, the Germans would stop people on the streets and take them as hostages in reprisal for real or supposed acts of resistance. They hustled them into trucks and drove them to gallows that had been erected all over Warsaw. The Germans stuffed the hostages' mouths with concrete so they could not shout "Long live Poland!" as they were being hanged.

One evening, as I was making my way down a dark street, I heard a low voice whisper, "Son, don't go any farther." I stepped into a doorway. As my eyes grew accustomed to the street, I noticed a light at the corner. German policemen in blue uniforms were seizing passers-by.

Getting enough to eat was a problem. The ration cards officially allowed us 669 calories a day. Even that amount of food was hard to obtain. The Germans weren't letting much food into the city. Once every two months, either my friend or I went to the country to get what we could from the farmers. If I was caught smuggling food in my suitcase or under the bandages which I wrapped around my arms, I would be killed.

As the atrocities increased, we decided that we had to fight back. Each student in the medical school became a member of the underground. A chain for the treatment of wounded Resistance fighters was set up.

"Zbigniew," my professor told me, "I want you to wait in this house, it's near the park." He marked down the address on a tiny piece of paper. "If a member of the underground is wounded in an action, someone will bring him to you. You must decide whether to treat him on the spot or send him to the hospital." He paused. "And here is another identification card. Your underground name is Zybszek Padlewski."

I was shocked. "But I'm only a medical student, not a doctor."

"We have to rely on students and professors. The Germans have murdered so many of our doctors." He turned to my friend. "You are to go to Ujazdowski Hospital after your anatomy class. Tell the Sister to list three men as being admitted to the hospital today. Tomorrow, after the action, the Nazis will check the hospitals to see if any wounded have been brought in. If they don't find any new listings, the men will be safe. Here are the documents with the false names that are to be written on the hospital records for today's entries."

The next morning, as I was dissecting a cadaver, the cleaning woman dropped a note that read "one P.M." in front of my wastebasket. I cleaned up and was on my way.

At the "safe" house, a kitchen table was covered with blankets and sheets. The cupboard held alcohol, whiskey, sheets torn into bandage-size pieces, and surgical tools.

At one-thirty, the door opened. A wounded soldier staggered over to the "operating table," and I examined his wound. "Just a bullet in the shoulder. Not too deep." I gave the man a swallow of whiskey. The morphine had to be saved for more serious cases. I removed the bullet and cleansed the wound.

The actions became so frequent that I began to take my textbooks to the medical station while I waited for the casualties.

As the Russians began to beat back the Germans, German officials became more and more afraid of our retaliatory tactics. Some of them became less vindictive. The underground had picked off each officer who was appointed head of the *Arbeitsamt*, the labor organization that sent Poles to Germany for forced labor. When a seventh man was appointed head of the *Arbeitsamt*, he sent a message to the underground. "I'd like to survive. I'll send only the elderly and volunteers to Germany." He kept his word and lived.

In April 1943, the Germans decided to "clean out" the Jewish ghetto. The Jews asked the Armia Krajowa to send them guns and to take part in the battle of the Warsaw Ghetto. The Polish underground sent ten ancient revolvers. Fearing there would be reprisals, the Polish government in exile refused to let the Armia Krajowa help the ghetto fighters. Though the poorly armed Jews fought valiantly for three weeks, German tanks and planes crushed the rebellion. In the end, only smoke and stones remained of a ghetto that had once housed half a million people.

Food became more and more scarce. The Germans stripped Polish farms of hams, cabbages, potatoes — anything to feed the German troops. The pressure built up as I tried to study, get enough to eat, and work with the underground. One day I was informed that a big action was being planned to attack Pawiak prison and liberate members of the Resistance. The action was to take place a few days before the most important exam in medical school. If you passed, you went on to your clinical work. If you failed, you had to repeat a whole year. I got permission not to take part in any actions for five days. With a kilo of potatoes and some fat, the only things that we could scare up for food, my friend and I holed up in a laboratory.

As we examined diseased organs and tissues, I wondered what I was doing in that room. Once we attacked Pawiak prison, we would be cut down or hunted like dogs. "What the hell," my friend said as he began to quiz me. "We've come this far, we might as well pass the exam."

159

The day before the exam, the plan to attack the prison was canceled. Too risky. The next day we passed the exam and drank a little laboratory-brewed *schnapps* to celebrate.

In 1943, we got word through the grapevine that the Germans planned to close the "sanitary school" and send all the workers and professors to concentration camps. Fortunately, that plan was canceled. I continued with my studies and working with the Resistance.

The summer of 1944 found the Russian troops approaching Warsaw. As the Germans started to move their families out of the city, we waited for the call to rise up and strike. Every Polish family had lost at least one member in a concentration camp or through public hangings. We wanted revenge.

Russian planes dropped leaflets: "Poles, rise up. Don't let the Germans get away." All around us, the pressure grew to strike.

Finally, on August 1, 1944, the Armia Krajowa gave the order: "Today, five P.M." My boss and I climbed into the German limousine that had been stolen and outfitted as an ambulance. Two stretchers reached along the length of the car. The driver headed for Wola, a section of the city, and the Karol and Marie hospital.

At five P.M. everyone poured onto the streets of Warsaw. Machine-gun fire cut down German soldiers strolling in the streets. Clusters of Molotov cocktails set tanks on fire. Armed with sticks and stones, the people of Warsaw joined the Resistance. The wounded began to arrive. I rushed from stretcher to stretcher.

At first, I treated wounded soldiers. Then the Germans

began to shoot anyone they found on the street, and there were civilian casualties as well.

The first few days, we had electricity and enough clean water to operate and cleanse the wounds. Then we had only battery-supplied electricity. Running water became a problem.

We kept waiting for the Russian troops on the other side of the Vistula to surge across the river and wipe out the Germans. We could see smoke rising from their campfires. Why didn't they help us? Thousands of Polish fighters had been killed in the Warsaw uprising. There was a shortage of pistols, machine guns, incendiary bombs, medical supplies. Where were our other allies? We looked to the skies. England was supposed to drop a Polish parachute brigade. Only American planes dropped ammunition and medicines. Our strongest weapons were a few German tanks captured in the first few days of the fighting.

Whole blocks of buildings collapsed as battles raged through the city and into Old Town. One morning, right after their breakfast, German pilots began to bombard Old Town. At lunchtime, they stopped. We dashed inside to pull out the wounded. After lunch, the bombers returned.

At the end of four weeks, thousands had been killed and we had run out of ammunition. Exhausted from sleepless nights and an epidemic of diarrhea, we knew the fight was lost.

A soldier entered the operating room, walking between the men and women lying shoulder to shoulder on the floor. "We've orders to evacuate the wounded. I'll lead you through the sewers to safety," he said.

My boss and I helped a wounded soldier hobble to the manhole. My body recoiled as the filthy water hit my chest. Exhausted from days and nights without sleep, I forced myself to push through the stench and debris. I would not give the Germans the satisfaction of dying.

"Keep going," the guide urged. "The point where we cut over to the sewer leading to the safe zone is only half a mile away."

Finally, I saw a pinpoint of light. Where did it come from? Were the Germans inside the sewer? Should we go forward?

"Don't stop now," the guide said. "We're almost there." He touched my friend on the shoulder. "You go first."

As my friend walked through the center of the sewer, the water rippled. There was a tremendous flash of light. Rocks tumbled all about us. I felt as though my head had been blown into fragments. The explosion cut off my friend's legs at the knees. The guide shoved the second man forward, "We've got to move quickly."

Another explosion. The man lay dead.

I was the fourth in line. The man in front of me walked toward the pinpoint of light.

Another explosion. The man lay dead.

"Are you afraid to go?" the guide asked me.

"Hell, yes. I don't know what's happening." What was my alternative? I couldn't go back. The other men had walked down the middle of the sewer and been killed. I pushed my back against the wall of the sewer and, moving sideward, avoided walking through the water in the middle of the sewer. Since I made no ripples, the Germans on top of the sewer didn't know I had passed.

I slipped back to recover my friend. Just then my boss

walked down the middle of the sewer. I heard the grenade drop, but it didn't explode. My boss crawled forward. "My back's broken. Carry me."

What should I do? The passage was too narrow for me to try to carry two people. "It's an order," my boss said. I had to put down my friend and pick up my boss.

For an hour I struggled forward. Finally, we reached the ladder leading to the manhole. I lifted the cover and saw the stars.

We spent the night in a safe house and then joined other freedom fighters trying to reach *Puszcza Kampinoska* (the Kampinoska Forest), just outside of Warsaw. By then, my boss discovered his back was not broken. He was able to walk unassisted. At one point, we spotted a German patrol. I began to cough. My boss stopped, handed me his scarf, and said, "Zbigniew, I order you to suffocate yourself to save everyone else."

I started to laugh and that stopped my coughing. He had ordered me to save his life, but mine was expendable! We dropped to the ground as the patrol passed. Ahead stood the unguarded German airport. No one expected Poles to be idiotic enough to attack their planes. We crawled under the wings, dashed across the runway into the woods and *Puszcza Kampinoska*.

The uprising was over. I fled to relatives in Czestochowa, about 65 miles north of Sosnowiec.

When the Russians entered Warsaw in January 1945, I returned. The beautiful building that had housed the medical school was now a pile of stone. A notice was posted on a fallen door, "Classes are now being held outside of Warsaw in an elementary school."

With great joy I made my way to the school and asked for my old professors.

"Most of them were killed or are missing in action." The registrar, a short man with a limp, tried to be helpful. "How can you prove you were enrolled in the school? Do you have any documents?"

"No, they were destroyed in the Warsaw uprising." To have survived all this and not be permitted to go to medical school!

The registrar rubbed his chin with his fingers. "What was the last exam you took?"

I grinned. "Anatomical pathology with Professor Ludwig Paszkiewicz. What a time I had studying for it!"

"Why, Professor Paszkiewicz is upstairs. Maybe he can help you."

I bounded up the stairs. The professor hugged me. "So, Zbigniew, you have survived. Now we must see if you are fit to go to medical school. Fortunately, the only thing I could save when my house caught fire was my notebook." He ran his finger over the list of those who had taken the exam. He smiled. "Congratulations. You passed with flying colors. Welcome back to the medical school."

In January 1947, I was awarded the degree of Doctor of Medicine. I had finally realized my dream of becoming a doctor.

Dr. Zbigniew Zawadzki was awarded the Cross of Valor and the Cross of Merit by the Polish government in exile (London, England) for his underground activities. For several years Dr. Zawadzki practiced medicine in Poland. In

1960, he decided to escape from Communist-occupied Poland with his wife and two small daughters. Dr. Zawadzki, a specialist in internal medicine and hematology, served as associate professor of medicine at Brown University in Rhode Island. He is an internationally acclaimed lecturer. His two daughters are doctors.

12

Dirk: Kidnaped for Forced Labor

... the raw material ... of the conquered
territories and their manpower are exploited
completely and conscientiously for the bene-
fit of Germany and her allies.

— Fritz Sauckel, Plenipotentiary General for
Mobilization of Labor, April 29, 1942

The outbreak of World War II caused a great shortage of labor in Germany. Most of the able-bodied men were either in the military services or in various government agencies like the Gestapo. Hitler had decided he did not want German women working in the factories. They were to stay home and raise children. Where was Germany to find the manpower to raise food and turn out guns and tanks?

The first answer was to use the thousands of Jews, Gypsies, political prisoners, and others who were imprisoned in the concentration camps in Germany. Millions of Polish Jews had been rounded up in ghettos in Poland. German armament firms were invited to set up plants nearby and make use of the "cheap labor" that could be rented from the S.S.

When the Germans invaded Russia on June 22, 1941, the need for additional laborers became even greater. By this time, more than a thousand concentration camps had been set up throughout Poland and Germany. Though Hitler had made the decision in 1941 to exterminate Jews and Gypsies, the S.S. convinced him to get every bit of labor out of the victims first. When the trainloads of victims arrived at the camps, the able-bodied men and women were separated from the others. These people were shipped to labor camps and worked until they were exhausted. Then they were sent to the extermination centers. Mothers, children, and the elderly had been sent directly to the gas chambers.

Political prisoners, prisoners of war, and captured resistance fighters also were forced to work in the war factories. The Russian prisoners of war were treated particularly badly. In the first few months of the Russian campaign, the Germans captured almost four million Russian prisoners. Hitler feared they would "infect" his people with communism and did not want to use them as laborers. They were herded into huge camps and allowed to die of disease and starvation. By early 1942, only about one million of the original four million Russian prisoners of war were still alive. By that time, German factories needed more and more workers, and Hitler permitted the use of Russian prisoners. The Russians were frequently selected at random and hanged to warn the other prisoners against attempting acts of sabotage.

All of the slave laborers suffered from lack of adequate food or water. Most died from hunger or disease. Their living conditions were terrible. At one work camp set up by the Krupp munitions firms, the prisoners slept in dog kennels.

As the war progressed, the supply of slave laborers taken from the concentration camps was not enough to meet the needs of the war industry. Germany first tried to recruit workers from the occupied countries. Skilled workers in Poland, Holland, Belgium, France, and elsewhere were asked to volunteer for labor in Germany. They were given false promises of good food and housing to entice them. Few volunteered.

The Germans then turned to forced recruitment. Soldiers marched into factories in occupied countries and took men from their workbenches. Men walking down the street or coming out of church would be seized and shipped off to Germany. By September 1944, millions of forced laborers from occupied countries were working in Germany. This included half a million Polish women who had been rounded up and sent to work as house slaves for German housewives.

In Russia, children from ten to fourteen years of age were rounded up by the German army. They were sent to German factories to work as apprentices and provide the slave labor of the future.

Though German firms made enormous profits from their use of slave labor, they have never admitted their guilt. Only a few have ever made any payments to the surviving slave laborers. Many of the slave laborers died from the terrible working and living conditions. Those who did survive continue to suffer mentally and physically from their brutal treatment.

Dirk, a Dutchman, was one of the millions sent to Germany.

———•—•———

The drone of the planes woke me up. I ran outside in my night clothes and looked across the water. The city of Rotterdam was in flames. Thousands of parachutists, like weird-looking mushrooms, floated down over the fields.

"Damned Germans," my father shouted, his nightcap falling off his head. "Why can't they leave us alone?"

Our island's only contact with the rest of the Netherlands was through our neighbor's radio. The whole village rushed to his door. He put the radio on the windowsill. It was May 10, 1940.

"German forces are attacking Dutch airfields and munitions dumps . . ." Abruptly the voice stopped. Our neighbor switched to the British Broadcasting Corporation. "Disregarding the Netherlands declaration of neutrality, Germany has attacked Holland."

If looks could kill, the German soldiers who landed on our island would have been dead before they walked off the docks. They marched to our city hall and lowered the Dutch flag. I spit as they replaced it with the swastika flag. They tacked signs on the bakery wall, on our post office, and at the entrance to our city hall. The signs read: "Be on the winning side. Join the German army." Spotlights appeared at each end of town. I got used to sleeping with the beams arching back and forth across my window as the Germans patrolled the skies for Allied planes.

My name is Dirk. I was sixteen and just finishing my three years at a trade school. In June 1940, I would begin my apprenticeship as a tool-and-die maker. I dreamed of going to America when I finished. Now this stupid war.

Every morning, my two brothers, Peter and Bert, and I pedaled our bikes to the tractor repair shop. When we finished, we helped in the garden. The garden was important because meat, eggs, and other foods were rationed.

In those days, even Peter, who was nineteen, didn't date. We spent our free time playing soccer or in boys' clubs that were run by the church.

Everyone seemed to accept the German occupation and went about their business. But on August 31, Queen Wilhelmina's birthday, every housewife washed the Dutch flag and hung it on the line to dry.

Secretly, we listened to the BBC on the radio our neighbor kept buried in his garden. On June 22, 1941, the BBC reported Hitler had invaded Russia. I was depressed. The swift victory we had hoped for vanished.

With millions of men at the front, Germany had a shortage of skilled laborers and agricultural workers. One morning, on our way to work, I stopped to chat with a friend. Bert and Peter rode ahead. As I waved goodbye to my friend, I noticed that German soldiers had pulled Peter and Bert off their bicycles. I ducked behind a door and watched as they were led down to the docks and put aboard a ship.

My happy, round-faced mother now had long moments of silence. She no longer sang as she scrubbed the family wash.

In July 1942, two German soldiers entered the shop where I worked. I kept my head down, not daring to look up from the lathe. Out of the corner of my eye, I saw them walk toward my bench. "*Du* (you)," they said, seizing my arm. I looked around. Nine other boys had been pulled from their lathes. "*Schnell, schnell* (faster, faster)" the soldiers shouted as they marched us toward the dock. Crowds gathered. A neighbor ran to get my mother. She thrust bread and cheese into my hands just as the boat cast off.

The boat docked in Rotterdam. The soldiers marched us

to the railway station and shoved us into wooden boxcars. I heard the bolt slam. Would I ever see my parents? My country? A slop bucket stood at one end of the windowless car. In a few hours, it overflowed. After two days, the stench from urine and feces clawed at my throat. I huddled against the wall, weak and nauseated.

When we reached Berlin, S.S. men pushed us onto a canvas-covered truck. Soon the noises of the city faded. My head began to clear as I smelled the aroma of pine trees. The truck stopped at Ebenswald, a labor camp. It was dusk, and the inmates were just returning to the barracks. The building reeked from the smell of a hundred unwashed men. There must really be a labor shortage to draft such elderly men.

An old man with reddish hair touched my arm. "Where are you from?"

"The Netherlands." Why couldn't he keep himself clean? How could the S.S. permit such filth?

Two of his teeth were missing and there was a fresh cut across his cheek. "My name is Jos. I was a medical student in Amsterdam. I've starving for news."

Medical student? He must be only a few years older than I. "How long have you been here?"

"Six months." He moved to make room for me on the wooden platform where I was to sleep next to five other men. "Tell me about Holland."

"My throat is dry and I'm starving," I loosened my shoelaces. "I haven't had anything to eat since yesterday. When's supper?"

"Here, there's no such word." He touched his swollen stomach. "We're fed at noon, slop."

My stomach cramped with fear and hunger. "How can they expect us to work on an empty stomach?"

"It's fatal to ask questions. And sleep with your arms around your boots." He looked at my sturdy shoes. His wooden clogs were stuffed with newspapers to make them fit. "Or they'll be stolen."

Before dawn the S.S. guards burst into the barracks. "*Raus, Raus* (out, out)." We lined up in groups of five as guards with German shepherd dogs by their sides checked the formation. If anyone stepped a little out of line, the dogs attacked.

At the factory, the guard shoved me in front of a workbench. "*Arbeit* (work)." He pointed to the blueprints for steam expanders for large pipes. S.S. guards patrolled the aisles, their whips lashing out at the workers. I stared at the blueprints, my head woozy from hunger. I was a stocky Dutchman, used to milk and cheese and butter. Fools, I wanted to shout. Feed a man properly, and you'll get twice as much work. The guard kicked the man next to me. "*Schnell, schnell.*"

I began to work the metal. At midday, a whistle sounded. I followed everyone outside. A prisoner ladled soup from a black kettle into small bowls. I stared at the few pieces of cabbage and potatoes and the piece of meat floating in the greasy water. The meat had maggots! A kitchen worker stuck a small square of bread in my hand.

"Eat," Jos said as he gulped down his food. "Eat if you want to see Holland again."

I took a spoonful. It smelled as though motor oil had been stirred into the soup. I forced down a spoonful. I spit it out. Then I bit into the small square of bread. Sawdust! I started to retch.

"You'll get used to it," Jos said as he licked his bowl. "This rotten soup is all that's between you and death."

One day, I got dizzy at my workbench. I had to lie down. If I did, I would be beaten to death. To go back to the barracks, I needed a pass from the factory manager. I knocked at Mr. Mueller's door. "I feel really sick. May I have a pass, please?"

"Come inside."

I stepped into the office. A tall, angular man whose broad face seemed to be dominated by his nose, Mr. Mueller was a civilian, not a member of the S.S. He began to speak Dutch. "Did you come of your own free will to Germany?" he asked.

"No!" What a stupid question.

"What do you think of Hitler?" His blue eyes peered at mine, as though he wanted an honest answer.

My face got red. "That bastard! He should go to hell." I banged my fist on the desk.

The manager jumped up, ran to the window, looked all around and slammed it shut. "You could have gotten us both killed. Don't ever say that. My wife comes from Belgium. I can understand your feelings, but I'm one of the few Germans who can." He handed me a pass.

I walked slowly back to the barracks. As I lay in the bunk, my stomach aching, I felt too weak even to pick the lice off my body. I had no future. Minutes earlier, the ever-present loudspeaker had announced, "Soldiers of our glorious Reich have captured the Russian naval base of Sevastopol. Rejoice. The day of total victory is near." There seemed to be no stopping the Germans, no way of striking back.

In 1943, all the men in my barracks were transferred to Fina, a factory adjacent to a German air base. We were a mixture of Dutch, French, Greek, and Polish forced laborers plus some English prisoners of war. In the same area, there was a special barracks that housed six hundred Russian prisoners of war. Though we worked in the same factory, we weren't permitted to talk to them.

One night, I was awakened by terrifying screams. In the morning, I saw laborers carting out the bodies of dead Russians. The guards had beaten them to death. What had initiated such barbarism? The guards began to gather in small groups, their faces pale and afraid.

Jos pulled his finger across his throat. "The Germans are finished. The Russians beat them at Stalingrad."

I stared at the falling snow. Was it possible that one day I would skate along the canals of Holland?

The Germans began to treat us a little better. They ladled out two rotten meals a day instead of one. Sometimes I was lucky enough to catch a rat or a bird to roast. Under our breath we made jokes about feasting on the guard's German shepherd.

Our underground network reported the Allies had taken Rome. Even on days when the swill stank, I forced myself to hold it down. I had to stay alive. I had to go back to Holland.

The only good thing about the camp was Ludmilla, the dark-eyed Polish girl who worked in the kitchen. I could see her from the factory window. Every day, she went behind the kitchen to dump sour milk. How I longed for that milk. The Germans didn't like sour milk, but they wouldn't give it to the starving prisoners. In a camp full of skeletons, Ludmilla looked like a woman, tall and buxom. The German cook permitted her to eat the scraps of food left on the plates of the German workers. They were given decent food.

Several men tried to get friendly with Ludmilla, offering her a stolen scarf or needle. She laughed and walked past them. One night, I started to cook some peas Mr. Mueller had given me. She passed by my little fire. I smiled. "Want to try my pea soup?"

"Pea soup?" She laughed. "You have a good imagination."

"No, smell it. The factory manager gave me some from his garden." I held up the spoon.

"Before the war, we had a vegetable garden and flowers, too," she said, as wistful as a little girl longing for a choco-late cookie in a bakery window.

"Come, sit and tell me about it." Although I never had had a girlfriend, I felt comfortable with her.

"We had roses, as soft and red as velvet. And oh, the scent." She sighed as if the roses infused the dusty air. "Roses and sweet peas, carrots and onions. How my father liked onions . . ." Her body began to tremble. I put my hand on her arm. She buried her face in my chest and sobbed.

Ludmilla began to hide the sour milk in a can under the porch. When no one was looking, I drank it. Was it love or the milk that gave me the energy to hope that I would see my country again?

Our factory was adjacent to an airfield and we got used

to Russian planes bombarding the area. One night, as we sat talking, the Russians began to drop flares. Ludmilla stood up.

I grabbed her by the wrist. "Don't go. The guards are hiding in the shelters." We huddled in the doorway, watching the burst of lights as the bombs hit their targets. As the bombing came closer, the rumble turned into sharp thuds. Despite their closeness, I was jubilant. "Soon we'll be free — free to go home."

Ludmilla's body turned limp. I grasped her to keep her from falling. "Home, for you." She shuddered. "For me — nothing, my mother, my father, my three sisters. Gone."

"How do you know that? You mustn't give up hope."

"I saw, with my own eyes. I was in the barn. I heard shots. I hid under the straw. At night, I found their bodies." She began to tremble. "For no reason, no reason."

"Ludmilla, come with me — marry me."

She shook her head. "I can't."

"Are you married?" Perhaps that was why she stayed away from the other men.

"No." She ran back to the barracks.

We had been hearing gunfire for several days. Each day, the sounds grew closer. One morning, before dawn, the guards shouted, "Out, out." They lined us up in groups of five and drove us down the road. I heard gunshots. The S.S. guards were shooting stragglers. I worked my way toward Ludmilla and grabbed her hand. When the guard turned to shoot a fallen prisoner, we fled into the woods. Finally, we had to catch our breath. We hid behind a huge tree until the column of prisoners and guards disappeared.

"Come on." I pulled her to her feet. We stumbled

through the forest, not knowing which way to go. Suddenly we came upon a paved road. A sign said, "Welcome to Neuruppin." Was it safe? I looked up and down. Abandoned tanks and trucks clogged the highway. We ran toward the houses, dashing from building to building. The houses seemed deserted. Suddenly, the door of a large house opened.

A small man with a waxed mustache stepped out and bowed as though we were visiting dignitaries. "Welcome. I am the mayor of Neuruppin." He looked at our ragged clothes. "The military base has been abandoned. The troops have fled. Come inside and have some cheese and milk."

After we ate, he took us to the deserted base. "You can stay here."

At the deserted barracks, Ludmilla stared at the neatly made cots. "Imagine, sheets and blankets." She started to cry.

Exhausted, we feel asleep. I began to dream of playing soccer with Peter and Bert.

Someone shook me.

I stared at the Russian soldier standing over me. His bayonet touched my chest.

"German?"

"*Nyet*. Dutch." I knew enough to pull out my Dutch passport slowly.

"Gun?"

"No, prisoner."

Ludmilla woke up. She looked at the soldier in his Red Army uniform. "The Russians are here! Thank God. '*Allevi*,' we are free."

The soldier turned and stared at her. "'*Allevi*'? *Du bist a Yid*? (You're Jewish?) Praise be to God. I thought my people had all been killed."

It was my turn to stare. "You're Jewish?" I asked Ludmilla.

She nodded, her throat swelling with tears. "Yes, that's why I can't marry you. I stayed alive only because I had false papers. I'm not Ludmilla Krakanova. I'm Sara Leah Goldberg."

"It doesn't matter; I want to marry you."

A few days later, the dapper mayor of Neuruppin performed the ceremony. A Russian lieutenant, who was Jewish, took us by truck to the American zone. We were to be exchanged for Russians who wanted to return to Russia. An American officer put us on a train with several hundred displaced persons.

The train taking us home was jammed with returning prisoners. As I sat on the windowsill, I saw the train move slowly past piles of stones that had once been buildings. The old world of lush green fields had turned to dust. Women driving horse carts filled with children and furniture tried to steer around the craters in the road. Everyone seemed to be trying to go somewhere, mostly away from Russian-occupied territory. The train came to a halt. The roadbed had been bombed.

It took six weeks by train, truck, and on foot to reach Nijmegen at the Dutch border.

The guard brushed aside my Dutch passport. "Take off your shirt, please." He inspected my armpits for the S.S. tattoo. "We can't be too cautious. Nazis with stolen passports have been trying to cross the border as Dutchmen. Welcome home."

After the war, Dirk and Sara lived in the Netherlands for eleven years. Through the World Council of Churches they arranged to come to America. Here, they raised three children. One of them, Sara proudly claims, "is eligible to be president since she was born in the United States."

13

André: The Slaves That Built the Rockets

The following asocial elements are to be transferred from the prison to the Reichsfuehrer S.S. to be worked to death: persons under protective arrest, Jews, Gypsies, Russians, Ukrainians, Poles . . . Czechs, and Germans with sentences of more than 8 years . . .

— Reichsfuehrer S. S. Himmler, September 18, 1942

During World War II, research on rockets was in its infancy. Instead of today's huge rockets that travel to the moon and the planets, scientists worked with rockets a few feet long. The United States army had the bazooka, a small antitank rocket that traveled only a few hundred yards. The Russian army used an artillery rocket that had a range of several miles.

In Germany, the story was different. There, Wernher von Braun was experimenting with a rocket 50 feet tall. It could carry a warhead of one ton and hit a city a hundred miles away. There was no defense against such a weapon.

Hitler did not take Wernher von Braun's rocket seriously until 1943. Up to that time, the war had been going well for the Germans. They thought they could win the war without new weapons. However, in 1943, the German armies had been defeated in Africa and Russia and were retreating. German cities were being pounded by American bombers during the day and by British bombers at night. Hitler was desperate for a weapon he could use against England. He had to prove to his people that the war was not lost. He now decided to use the new secret weapons his scientists were developing. The German army and the German air force competed with each other to supply those weapons.

The army's weapon was the V-2 (*V* for Vengeance), Wernher von Braun's rocket. The air force was working on a weapon called the V-1. The V-1 was perfected first. It was a pilotless aircraft with a range of approximately a hundred miles and could carry a one-ton load of explosives in its nose. In 1944, V-1 launchings started in France. They were initially successful in striking targets in Great Britain. However, the V-1 could be shot down by fighter planes and antiaircraft cannon or snared in cables suspended from barrage balloons. It soon ceased to be effective.

The V-2 was a much more dangerous weapon. It ascended high into the stratosphere and came down at supersonic speed. There was no way of destroying it.

Hitler ordered Wernher von Braun to perfect the V-2 as soon as possible. Wernher von Braun set up facilities to produce and test the rocket at Peenemunde on the north coast of Germany. Peenemunde is on a peninsula that juts out into the Baltic Sea. When the rockets were assembled, they were test fired out over the water where they could be tracked.

The British air force had noticed that something was going on in Pennemunde, but they weren't sure what it was. Their aerial photographs showed long silver cylinders, but they could not believe these were rockets because they were so much bigger than British rockets. Finally, the British decided that something very dangerous was happening at Pennemunde. During the night of August 17, 1943, hundreds of British bombers struck Pennemunde and wiped out the facility. Many of Germany's top rocket scientists were killed in the raid.

Hitler was furious. He wanted his vengeance weapon and he wanted it quickly. He moved the production of the V-2 to underground caverns where it would be safe from bombing attacks. The Harz Mountains, in the center of Germany, were selected for the site of the rocket-assembly plant.

The Harz Mountains contained minerals and had been mined for hundreds of years. But the existing mine shafts were too small to be used for rocket assembly, so they had to be enlarged to heights of 40 to 90 feet.

This meant drilling into solid rock; hard and dangerous work. Where would the workers come from? Heinrich Himmler, the head of the S.S., offered the use of slave labor from the concentration camps. There was an endless supply of Jews, Gypsies, political prisoners, prisoners of war, and resistance fighters. They could be worked to death; then new supplies of slave labor would replace them. A special labor camp, called Dora, was set up for the V-2 project. At first the prisoners both worked and slept in the damp, dust-filled underground caverns. They worked in twelve-hour shifts, clawing out the stone with hammers, picks, and shovels. They slept in crude wooden bunks set up in the damp, noisy tunnels. Once a week they were taken outside.

The laborers died like flies from the brutal work, the poor food, and the unhealthy living conditions. Prisoners were beaten to death for the slightest reason. Many were hanged to serve as a warning for other prisoners not to slacken their work. Of the 60,000 prisoners who were forced to work on the V-2 project at Dora, 30,000 died.

By 1944, Dora was producing V-2 missiles for testing. By the spring of 1945, the missiles were used to attack England, with a terrifying effect. Without warning, a missile would crash on a city, and a ton of explosives would destroy everything for hundreds of feet. Fortunately, the Allied troops had by this time invaded Europe. They captured the V-2 launching sites in Holland and Belgium soon after the first rockets had been launched.

By April 1945, Allied troops had captured the V-2 assembly site at Dora. The S.S. had removed the prisoners working there and many were massacred.

After World War II, the United States brought Wernher von Braun and his fellow rocket scientists to America to help start its space program. Today, as Americans watch the spectacular rocket launchings, few are aware of the program's tragic beginning in a place of hunger, exhaustion, and death called Dora. André Gerard was among the few who survived to tell his story.

"*Mesdemoiselles et messieurs* . . ." The professor interrupted his lecture. Everyone turned toward the door and the sound of footsteps on the stairs.

I stood up and looked out the window. German soldiers and dogs surrounded the horseshoe-shaped courtyard of the university. If I jumped out the third-story window, I'd land on the Germans. The door burst open.

"Against the wall." The sergeant pointed his gun at us. The other soldiers did a body search. "All right, everyone outside."

In the courtyard, Georges Mathieu, a member of the Resistance, was talking to the S.S. Georges a traitor? He was the one who had recruited me into the Resistance in 1941. Georges gave me my false identification papers. He knew my real name.

It was November 25, 1943. How foolish I had been to return to Clermont-Ferrand. Last June, when other students in the Resistance had been arrested, I fled to the mountains. By October, I thought it would be safe to come back. I didn't want to miss a year of school. The Germans were losing on the Russian front, and I thought the war would be over in a few months.

Since 1940, I had been trying to evade the Germans. For an Alsatian, it was a natural reaction. From the cradle, I had been raised with, "*Vice la France et mort aux Boches* (Long live France, and death to the Germans)." Over the centuries, my region of Alsace-Lorraine had alternated between German and French rule. After World War I, it again became French. In May 1940, when France capitulated, the Germans reclaimed it. They began to draft men from Colmar, my hometown, into the German army. My brother-in-law and several cousins were taken.

I was almost eighteen. I wasn't going to fight for the enemy or stay in occupied territory. One Sunday afternoon, I climbed on my bicycle, pedaled south to the Swiss border, and crawled under the fence into Switzerland. The Swiss police handed me over to the French consul.

"So, André Gerard, what do you suggest we do with you?" the consul asked, eyeing the dozens of other young Frenchmen in the waiting room.

"Please help me to reach unoccupied France. Arrange for me to go by way of Geneva to Lyon. Then I can make my way to Clermont-Ferrand. The University of Strasbourg has been evacuated to there. I want to study law."

In a short while I was on the train. I arrived in Clermont-Ferrand as the church bells pealed four A.M. Where does one go in a dark, strange city? I followed the chimes to the cathedral. After mass, I approached the priest and asked, "Father, can you help me? I'm looking for some students who escaped from Alsace."

"Follow me." He led me outside just as dawn began to filter into the city. At the dormitory, I embraced my former classmates who had fled to Clermont-Ferrand.

Like so many of the other anti-Nazi students who had fled from Alsace, I soon joined the Resistance movement, COMBAT. There, I learned the first rule of the Resistance: "If the Resistance asks you to do something, don't ask questions." The less one knew, the less likelihood, if caught, of betraying others.

At first, my work with the Resistance involved sneaking out during the curfews to print and distribute *Combat*, the underground newspaper. But when the Allies invaded North Africa in late 1942, the Germans took over the so-called unoccupied zone of France. German troops occupied Clermont-Ferrand.

From propaganda the Resistance went to sabotage. Sometimes, the order would come down from the high command: "Rendezvous at point X. When the Cathedral of Clermont-Ferrand strikes two, light the fuse. Then disappear." Or, if there was to be a parachute drop in the mountains, "Stand at the crossroads. Keep a lookout." As soon as we heard the motor of a plane, another member of the Resistance lit a flare. Others picked up the arms and carried them into the woods. Sometimes we guided to safety a parachutist sent by General Charles de Gaulle to work with the Resistance.

But now, a prisoner of the Germans, I stood facing Georges Mathieu. What would they do with me? I thought of my sweetheart, Simone. Would I see her again?

"Your identification papers," Georges demanded.

I stared at him with contempt and handed him the forged documents he had given me.

"Not these, you fool. Give me your real papers."

"These are my real papers," I insisted. "I'm Jean Matisse from Lille."

"Don't make a fool of me. Give me the real ones."

"These are the only papers I have."

He turned to the Gestapo agent and said in German, "This fellow is very dangerous, put him aside."

That bastard! I came from Alsace and spoke German as fluently as I spoke French. I pretended not to understand.

No matter how many times the Gestapo slapped me in the face, I kept insisting I was Jean Matisse from Lille. That night — I can never forget the date, November 25, 1943 — they took me to the military prison. The S.S. threw me into a cell with eight other prisoners.

The next morning, the Gestapo resumed the interrogation. The room was barren except for a desk and a few chairs. Despite the blows, I kept repeating, "I'm Jean Matisse from Lille." But when the man who was translating my answers from French into German made a mistake, I corrected him.

"So, you do speak German?" the Gestapo lieutenant snapped.

"A little."

"You are in fact, André Gerard, from Colmar, in Alsace." He slapped me across the mouth. His assistant pulled out a file marked "André Gerard." They had known all along who I was.

A few days later, with a number of other prisoners, I was shipped to Compiègne, an assembly point north of Paris. Pierre Bayard, an Englishman whose mother was French, was in the group. I was the only one who knew that his real name was Peter Beech. He was really a British officer and had been parachuted into France.

For two months our routine consisted of interrogations, work details, and roll calls.

On January 24, 1944, our group of two thousand French prisoners was herded into cattle cars, a hundred to a car. The doors swung shut. We heard a loud click as the guard bolted the door. Convoy #42 000 moved toward its destination. I looked around the jammed car. There was no food, water, toilets, or windows. For some unfathomable reason, the Germans had given us back the belongings they had taken when we were arrested. Sandwiched inside my notebook was my pocketknife. Those of us who had knives began to cut into the wooden floorboards. Despite the guards and dogs, it might be possible to escape.

When our fingers became numb from the cold others took the knives and went on trying to loosen the boards. After a few hours, my head was dizzy from the stink of urine and lack of ventilation. Finally, in Trier, Germany, the train stopped. The door clanged open.

"*Raus, raus*, there's water at the spigot." The guards swung at us with their "gummies," electric cables covered with rubber. What kind of monsters were they? They couldn't give us an order without blows to our heads and backs. As we tried to gulp down enough water to replenish our dehydrated bodies, the guards inspected the cars.

"Swine," they shouted, striking us with their gummies, "there is no escape." They shoved us into another boxcar, which was practically airtight. From then on, each moment became a struggle for breath.

After two days, the train stopped. "*Raus, raus* (get out, get out), *schnell, schnell* (fast, fast)," the guards shouted as they opened the door. Many of my companions were unable to rise. In the airless car, they had suffocated to death. The survivors had to line up and march through the gate of the camp. A sign reading, "*Jedem das Seine* (Each Gets What He Deserves)" hung above the gate. We had arrived at Buchenwald.

"To the showers," the guards shouted. Couldn't they ever speak in a normal voice? (At that moment, we were unaware of the other meaning of the word *showers*. Gas chambers were labeled "showers" to disguise their real purpose.) We ran forward.

"Take off all your clothes," the guard said. "You, go to the barber on your left."

The barber shaved our heads and all the hair on our bodies. We looked at each other. Suddenly, we were no longer the persons we had known but grotesque strangers. When I came out of the shower, my clothing had disappeared. Instead of my leather shoes, I got a pair of wooden clogs and a torn shirt, pants, and a coat. Still naked, and shivering from the cold, I had to sew a red patch with a number, 42 028, on the pants and one on my shirt. As a political prisoner, I ceased to be André Gerard. I was only 42 028. In the eyes of the Germans, I became a "piece," or *stueck*, the property of the S.S., no longer human.

That night, I slept on the top tier of a bunk, like a log of wood piled next to the others. The next morning, I stared at the 500 other prisoners who had arrived in earlier shipments. They looked like walking skeletons.

In the morning, the whole camp lined up on the *appell-platz* (the assembly area). Once, twice, three times, the Germans counted and recounted as we stood there in the freezing rain, our bodies weak from lack of food. After roll call, the S.S. marched us to the stone quarries.

"Line up, two by two. Together, lift the stones onto planks and drag them up the stairs. Anyone caught shirking will be killed." In our exhausted condition, it seemed an impossible task. Out of the corner of my eye, I saw a man pause to rest; the guard beat him to death. At that moment, I couldn't imagine that one day I would look back on Buchenwald as an "easy" camp.

One morning the guard entered the barracks and

shouted, "42 028" and a hundred other numbers. We were marched to a waiting truck. The truck sped over the bumpy roads. The driver stopped only for the guards to go to the bathroom or to eat their lunch. In the evening, we came to what appeared in the darkness to be a camp.

To shouts of *"raus, raus, schnell, schnell"* the guards raised their gummies, driving us into a barracks. "Lie down on the floor and go to sleep."

We had arrived at Dora. The next morning, during the roundup on the *appellplatz*, we could see snow-covered hills surrounding a small valley. Beyond the hills were trees. Only a few of the barracks had been completed. Several were under construction. When the guards finally finished their interminable counting, they shouted, "Forward march." A gate opened, and we followed the railroad tracks leading inside the mountain.

Like gnomes, we vanished into a tunnel. At first, it was hard to comprehend the size of this labyrinth beneath the Harz Mountains. The inside of the mountain was crisscrossed with tunnels. As we marched, we saw that the main tunnels stretched from one side of the mountain to the other.

In the dim light of randomly scattered electric bulbs, we saw some prisoners drilling with jackhammers, while others scratched with picks and shovels to enlarge the caverns and build new ones. They kept their heads down, not looking up as we passed. The guards kicked aside the bodies of workers who had fallen dead from exhaustion. I started to choke as the dust from the jackhammers invaded my lungs. Charles Sadron, a physics professor, stood beside me.

"Charles, we are not going to survive a month in this place," I whispered.

"My God, you're an optimist. We won't last a week."

What could I do to stay alive?

Finally, at the far end of the tunnel, we reached Hall Zero, the administration building.

"Line up in twos," the guards shouted. "The first two, into the office."

As each twosome came out, we asked, "What happened?"

"The Germans want to know what we did in civilian life."

I turned to Charles Sadron. "You're okay, you're a professor of physics, but I know they have no use for a law student. They'll make me dig tunnels until I die. But I have one advantage. I speak German and you don't. When they ask you a question, look puzzled. I'll ask if I can interpret for you. After that, just say '*Ja.*'"

When our turn came, the civilian in charge of personnel asked, "You," pointing at Charles, "what did you do?"

Charles looked at me.

"If you would permit me, sir, my friend does not speak German. I will interpret for him. Permit me to present Professor, Doctor, Engineer Charles Sadron of the University of Strasbourg, a professor of physics."

"*Gut, gut.* He is assigned to Commando 185. Sawatski Commando, a great honor."

"And what did you do?" the interrogator asked me.

"I was his student, his laboratory assistant at the University of Strasbourg," I lied. If they ever checked my records at the university, I was dead.

"Is this true?" the German asked Professor Sadron.

"*Ja.*" Charles, too, would be dead if they found out he had lied.

"You will continue to work with him. Sawatski Commando 185, Hall 28."

Little did Charles Sadron and I know that we had drawn the most prized assignment in this nightmare called Dora. We were to make the final checkout of the "*mischgerat.*" No one told us what was in this black box that came sealed with a swastika. But I picked up from conversation between the Austrian and German civilians supervising the assembly that the Germans were building a secret weapon. These civilians thought that even though I knew German, I was French and too stupid to understand what was going on. The A-4, later called the V-2 rocket, *V* for Vengeance, was to be Hitler's means of winning the war. This rocket's range would be great enough to wipe out the cities of Great Britain.

Our job was to check the *mischgerat* for each rocket. The *mischgerat* was the brains of the rocket. It controlled all the guidance systems. If the *mischgerat* did not work properly, the rocket could not be guided to its target.

"You are never, never to open this box, understand?" the civilian engineers in charge of Hall 28 kept telling us.

Charles Sadron and I began our daily, 24-hour-long existence as moles. Hall 28, beneath the green hills of the Harz Mountains, like all of the other 46 halls, was constantly filled with dust. The gray film from the excavations drifted, covering each inch of space. It clawed at our throats and made us gag. It covered our lice-infested straw pallets and thickened our soup. The water that constantly dripped from the rocks filled the hall with dampness. The emptiness in our stomachs, the noise from the jackhammers, the stench from the barrels that served as our latrine, and the idiotic din of the engineer who endlessly rang his bell as he drove his train around the track, permeated our entire bodies.

The two-mile path to the exit was strewn with dead bodies. As fast as they were removed, new prisoners arrived to take their place. At first, the Germans shipped the bodies back to Buchenwald to be burned. Then, to be more efficient, they built their own crematorium at Dora. The sickening smell of burning flesh invaded the caverns.

One day, the head supervisor announced, "Since we're checking the most important element in the rockets, we have to keep it safe from dust. Even if the mechanism checks out properly, a few particles of dust could distort it in flight."

The next thing we knew, we were constructing a room inside Hall 28. We were delighted. Now, when the S.S. came to check on us, they had to open a door. It gave us just enough warning to look busy. Our job really didn't require much knowledge of physics, so I was fairly certain I wouldn't be discovered as a fraud.

But one day, a group of civilians, led by a general, entered the room. I became more apprehensive than usual. Still, I was intrigued that the brass would actually venture inside this hellhole. The civilians began to scrape and bow. One of them turned to a tall, well-built, blond-haired man and nodded at Charles.

"Herr von Braun, may I present the noted physicist, Professor, Doctor, Engineer Charles Sadron of the University of Strasbourg."

"As a student, I read some of your papers, Dr. Sadron,"

the man said. "I am sorry that we meet under these circumstances."

"And I."

The officials completed their inspection and left.

"Who was he?" I asked as the door closed.

"Wernher von Braun, the genius behind the German rocket program," Charles said.

One of the Germans, Herr Krueger, played his radio on high all day long, but the moment the one o'clock news came on with its military announcements, he turned it down. I usually tried to be near him at one P.M., but it was hard to hear with the volume lowered.

One day, Krueger's radio went "*kaput* (broken)." All morning he paced back and forth across the floor. Finally, he came to me. "42 028, aren't you a radio engineer?"

"But of course," I said, wondering how I could get out of this one.

"Will you check my radio for me?"

I gave him a big smile. "My pleasure. Leave it here, and I'll see what I can do. Discreetly, of course. Our secret." A friend of mine on the night shift had owned a radio shop in Clermont-Ferrand. I'd pass it on to him.

The next morning, as the shifts changed, my friend told me, "A tube is burned out. You need a new one."

For weeks Krueger looked all over the town of Nordhausen for a new tube. None to be had.

"Herr Krueger, I know where to find a tube." I said, watching him pace back and forth in distress.

"Where?" he asked, already knowing the answer.

"Inside the *mischgerat*."

"You'll be hanged for that," he whispered.

"Okay," I said. "I don't need the tube."

A few days later, he sidled up to me. "What would you do with the rest of the box?"

"Herr Krueger, corpses disappear inside the mountain. Why not a box?"

The pacing continued. Finally he said, "I have a two-day leave. It would be nice if my radio worked when I came back."

When he returned, Herr Krueger turned the dial and got music. At one P.M., when he turned down the daily news broadcast, I stood next to him. "A little louder, Herr Krueger. I can't hear." Blackmail, of course.

By May 1944, barracks had been completed outside the tunnels. We now slept there and marched back and forth to work.

On June 6, 1944, I heard the thrilling news that the Allies had landed in Normandy. "This is it, boys, we'll soon be going home."

As punishment for the Allied invasion, the Germans immediately cut our meager rations. Our lives outside the tunnel became an unrelenting routine of standing at attention, beatings, and the threat of being selected for the increased random hangings.

Still, with the news of the Allied advance, we began to have hope. On Bastille Day, July 14, 1944, as we walked into the tunnel, a voice broke out in the "Marseillaise." Our voices swelled, as the words echoed through the tunnels:

> "*Allons enfants de la patrie*
> "*Le jour de gloire est arrivé . . .*
> (*Forward, our sons of our country*
> *The days of glory are here . . .)*"

As we finished, the group of Russian prisoners in front of us began to sing, "To Moscow, to Moscow . . ."

At the sound of the singing, the S.S. rushed to the main tunnel and fell upon the Russians with their gummies.

Toward the end of August I heard glorious news. The Allies were only eighty miles from the Rhine River. "Hey, we'll be home by September," I told Charles Sadron.

In the meantime, we were given an additional job: to inspect and adjust some new control instruments, which contained a pendulum. "My" Austrian emphasized the importance of this new gadget when he told me about it. "If it does not work, the rocket goes 'pfft,' and falls down. It must always turn toward the target. We wouldn't want to miss the target, would we?"

"How can we tell if it won't work?" I asked, as seriously as possible.

"*Ach*, that is the problem. You cannot tell until you shoot it up. A terrible tragedy."

"*Ja*, a terrible tragedy. I will translate your words exactly into French. Hey, guys," I said, switching to French. "Don't laugh. This joker says the rocket won't work if we don't make the pendulum checks exactly right. And the only way to test it is in operation."

"Remember," the Austrian said. "It would be a tragedy to miss the target."

"*Quel dommage!*" The Frenchmen nodded. "What a shame."

One afternoon, all hell broke loose. The S.S. and a number of army officers stormed into the underground plant. "Stop! Line up! Prisoners on one side, civilians on the other."

The civilians turned white.

The S.S. slapped me against the wall. "Someone is trying to sabotage the war effort."

Would they interrogate me and find out I didn't know anything about electronics? I stood there, frozen.

The gummies fell on everyone. After an hour of questioning, satisfied that we were not the culprits, they left. I later overheard that the soldiers who made the last checks of the V-2 before it left the plant were executed. They had failed to detect that some of the instruments had been sabotaged or improperly assembled.

At the end of March 1945, Herr Krueger turned green as Radio Berlin reported, "The American army has crossed the Rhine at Remagen. Every German man, woman, and child must fight to the death." The top S.S. began to disappear. Older, less fanatic men now guarded us. Every day as we stood on the *appellplatz* to be counted and recounted, we heard artillery fire. I said my Hail Marys and prayed. "Lord, let me live and return to France."

Overhead, hundreds of American Flying Fortress bombers thundered toward their German targets. What a beautiful, beautiful sight. I felt as though the heavens had opened up. It was as though I were hearing the hymn at the end of Beethoven's Ninth Symphony. Now at last, I could be a human being.

Fighter pilots, their escort service accomplished, veered off to zoom down and machine-gun the steam engines sitting in the nearby freight yard. The German bastards were finally getting a taste of their own medicine.

One day, we were not allowed out of the tunnel. An argument seemed to be going on between the civilians and the S.S. We didn't find out until later that Himmler, the head of the S.S., had given orders to kill all the slaves who had worked on the V-2 rocket. He didn't want any information about Germany's secret weapon to fall into Allied hands. He didn't want us to live, either, to testify about Nazi brutality.

Then, on April 1, the S.S., with their usual, "*Raus, Raus, schnell, schnell,*" made us run out of the tunnel and into a string of boxcars. They handed each of us a piece of bread and shoved 130 prisoners into each boxcar. The train pulled out, destination unknown. The next day, the train stopped short. The tracks had been destroyed by Allied bombers.

"Out, form rows of five." The guards marched us through the mountains, freely swinging their gummies to keep us moving. Those who fell behind were shot. Despite two years of starvation, I willed myself to walk. I thought about France, my parents, my sweetheart Simone. My time to die had passed.

At the next town, the S.S. found another train. On we went and every so often, we heard the sound of fighter planes overhead. The train stopped. The S.S. ran into the brush, pointing their machine guns at the cattle car so we could not escape. Every time we heard the whine of a plane as it peeled off to inspect the train, we trembled. Fortunately, the pilots checked again and again to see who was inside. Not once did they bomb or strafe the cattle cars.

Finally, we arrived in Ravensbruck, a women's camp. The women had been evacuated. I couldn't believe my eyes when the Germans handed us Red Cross packages. We hadn't eaten in three days. We tore open the bars of chocolate and pried open the cans of Spam and gulped them down.

A few days later, I woke up before dawn. Absolute silence for the first time in days! Minutes later, a tremendous barrage of artillery fire in the south. The Russians had unleashed their last — and victorious — offensive, against Berlin. It was the last battle of the war.

As the sounds of mortars and artillery fire grew closer to Ravensbruck, the S.S. marched us westward to escape from the Russians. The roads from the east were jammed with German civilians and soldiers trying to flee from the advancing Soviet army. Suddenly we were caught by an advanced Russian unit. Chaos broke out as a group of die-hard S.S. men dashed out of the woods and returned the Russian fire.

Everyone — our guards, the civilians, prisoners — ran as fast as we could to escape the crossfire. In the confusion, Pierre Bayard, who had been a prisoner at Dora, and I became separated from the others.

We entered a little village. Just ahead, truckloads of German soldiers, tanks and foot soldiers with their arms over their heads, filled the road. Around the bend stood a huge Russian tank, its gun pointed at the Germans. "Surrender or else." What a beautiful sight! The Russian soldiers looked no more than sixteen or seventeen years old.

"*Tovarich, tovarich* (comrades, comrades)," we screamed. "*Frantzuski* (French)."

The Russians welcomed us and offered us something to drink. That night, we slept in a barn. The next day we found the Russians had set up roadblocks. Though the Allies were only three kilometers away, the Russians wouldn't let us go west.

"I'll be damned," I said to Pierre. "Just follow me." I went through the door of a house and climbed out the back window onto a small path. By skirting the main roads, we reached Ludwigslust, and met our first American.

He staggered drunkenly across the road. Across his chest, like a giant necklace, hung seven S.S. daggers. In his right hand, he waved a tremendous cavalry saber, slashing out at imaginary enemies. We ducked and came to another American leaning on a jeep.

Pierre, who spoke English, shouted, "Hallo, we're Frenchmen, prisoners."

Within a few days, we found ourselves on a train with Frenchmen who had worked as forced laborers in Germany. They stared at our skeletal frames and shaved heads. As the train rolled through Belgium toward France, I turned to Pierre, my voice choking. "Pierre, we're going back to France and we won't even know when we're actually crossing the border."

When we approached a tiny village, the train slowed almost to a stop. The stationmaster waved a newspaper: GERMANY CAPITULATES. "*Vive la France* (Long live France)!" It was May 8, 1945. V-E Day, Victory in Europe.

At the town of Hazebrouck, government relief workers handed us our first clean clothes in over a year. Each man received a printed postcard: "Have arrived in France. In good health. See you soon." I signed the card and addressed it to my parents in Colmar. They would write my sweetheart, Simone, in Clermont-Ferrand. Would she still be waiting for me?

The next day, we arrived in Paris! Mobs of people filled the platform waving placards at us. Some had photographs, others bore signs reading, "Have you seen _____ " or, "Did you know so-and-so?" People followed us to the hotel and crowded the sidewalk and steps. There was no mistaking the survivors of Dora. We were walking skeletons. An army officer knocked at the door of the room in which Pierre and I were quartered.

"Did you know my son?" he asked, mentioning a name. "He was a student at Clermont-Ferrand."

We were silent. How could we tell a father his son had died of starvation during the last days of the war? Finally, Pierre said as gently as possible. "Your son died at Ravensbruck."

"Are you sure?"

We nodded. "We both saw the body."

The next day, he came back. "Are you sure? I haven't had the courage to tell his mother."

We nodded. He softly closed the door.

A few days later, I boarded the train to Colmar. What would I find? Were my parents still alive? My sister? Had they heard from Simone?

As I stepped off the train, I heard my mother shout, "André!"

Since they received my postcard, my mother and sister had been meeting every train from Paris.

The three of us stood there sobbing. Finally, my sister was able to speak. "I had a letter from Simone. She's waiting for you in Clermont-Ferrand."

After the war, André Gerard returned to Clermont-Ferrand to obtain his law degree. He and Simone have five children and several grandchildren. In 1948, he came to

America and earned a degree in American law. He has had a distinguished career as an international lawyer. His sister's husband, who had been drafted into the German army, deserted. He had managed to join the Free French Fighting forces and had taken part in the Allied invasion of southern France in August 1944.

Postscript

The numbers of those murdered by the Nazis, six million Jews and five million other victims, are hard to believe. How can we be sure this really happened?

First, there are the records, photographs, and movies captured from the German army. In carefully written ledgers, the Germans documented their crimes: time, place, method, and numbers. The records today are in the National Archives of the United States in Washington, D.C.

There are the testimonies of the men and women who committed the crimes. They were tried in Nuremberg, Germany, after World War II for "crimes against humanity."

There are the personal stories of Jews and Christians who, by a miracle, managed to survive the horrors of slave labor or the death camps.

There are the documents discovered in the ruins of the Warsaw Ghetto. During the Nazi occupation, Emmanuel Ringelbaum, a doomed Jewish historian, collected diaries, letters, underground newspapers, and drawings and placed them in sealed metal containers. The contents of these buried time capsules record the methodically planned destruction by the Nazis: the day-by-day starvation in the ghettos, the slave labor, and the shipment of millions of people in cattle cars to the gas chambers. The writers prayed, as they themselves went to their deaths, that these records would be discovered and read by future generations.

There are the testimonies of the Allied soldiers who accidentally came upon the camps. The Allied troops had moved across Europe so quickly that the Germans did not have time to destroy the evidence of their crimes. When General George Patton's Third Army entered Ohrdruf concentration camp, they discovered over three thousand corpses that had been thrown into shallow graves. Other corpses lay where they had fallen. The few survivors of the camp were walking skeletons.

General Patton, a hardened warrior, was so shocked that he immediately notified General Dwight D. Eisenhower, Supreme Commander of Allied Forces in Europe. With Generals Patton and Omar Bradley, Eisenhower inspected the camp. As they inspected the gas chambers, the crematorium, the torture room, Eisenhower turned white. Patton threw up. Bradley was too stunned to speak.

Eisenhower issued orders that every American unit in the area visit Ohrdruf. "We are told that the American soldier does not know what he is fighting for. Now, at least, he will know what he is fighting against."

Despite Eisenhower's testimony, hate groups now are trying to tell us the Holocaust never happened.

Why are these hatemongers attempting to tell us the Holocaust is a myth? Why are they preaching anew the

Nazi theory of Aryan superiority? Like Hitler, they too have dreams of ruling the world. Their claim of racial purity and the goal of eliminating only one or two groups of "inferior peoples" are lies. Their aim is to control the world and to enslave others.

The flames of hatred are easy to ignite, especially against someone of another color or another religion. It is easy to deny an event that happened fifty years ago. People want to forget the horrors of the past.

But we cannot. The six million Jews and five million others were scientifically, deliberately murdered by the Nazis. Millions of other lives were disrupted, either physically or mentally. Millions more were killed on the battlefields and in the bombing of cities. The Holocaust *did* happen in the "civilized" twentieth century. It was not accomplished by Hitler alone. It was carried out by educators, scientists, doctors, lawyers, and every segment of German society. Ordinary citizens helped to make it happen.

The Holocaust poses a warning and a challenge to each of us. Like the young people whose stories are told in this book, each of us has a responsibility to safeguard the rights of others. If we do not, our own rights could vanish.

Other Books of Interest to the Reader

Cowan, Lore. *Children of the Resistance.* New York: Archway Books, 1971.

Finkelstein, Norman. *Remember Not to Forget.* New York: Watts, 1985.

Forman, James. *The Survivor.* New York: Farrar, 1976.

Frank, Anne. *Anne Frank: The Diary of a Young Girl.* New York: Doubleday, 1967.

Friedman, Ina R. *Escape or Die: True Stories of Young People Who Survived the Holocaust.* New York: Harper, 1982.

Greene, Betty. *Summer of My German Soldier.* New York: Dial, 1973.

Kerr, Judith. *When Hitler Stole Pink Rabbit.* New York: Coward, 1971.

Kerr, M.E. *Gentlehands.* New York: Harper, 1978.

Koehn, Ilse. *Mischling, Second Degree.* New York: Greenwillow, 1977.

Leitner, Isabella. *Fragments of Isabella: A Memory of Auschwitz.* New York: Crowell, 1978.

Meltzer, Milton. *Never to Forget: The Jews of the Holocaust.* New York: Harper, 1976.

Murray, Michele. *The Crystal Nights.* New York: Seabury, 1973.

Orgel, Doris. *The Devil in Vienna.* New York: Dial, 1978.

Orlev, Uri. *The Island on Bird Street.* Boston: Houghton Mifflin, 1984.

Plant, Richard. *The Pink Triangle: The Nazi War Against Homosexuals.* New York: Holt, 1986.

Ramati, Alexander. *And the Violins Stopped Playing: A Story of the Gypsy Holocaust.* New York: Watts, 1986.

Reiss, Johanna. *The Upstairs Room.* New York: Harper/Crowell, 1972.

Richter, Hans P. *Friedrich.* New York: Penguin/Puffin, 1987.

Rogasky, Barbara. *Smoke and Ashes: The Story of the Holocaust.* New York: Holiday, 1988.

Spiegelman, Art. *Maus.* New York: Pantheon, 1973.

Suhl, Yuri. *They Fought Back: The Story of the Jewish Resistance in Nazi Europe.* New York: Schocken, 1967.

Wiesel, Elie. *Night.* New York: Bantam, 1981.

Ziemian, Joseph. *The Cigarette Sellers of Three Crosses Square.* Minneapolis: Lerner, 1970.

Index

211